Abby Guy

Race and Slavery on Trial in an 1855 Southern Court

by
Russell Mahan

Published by Historical Enterprises
2780 Bella Sol Drive
Santa Clara, Utah 84765
HistoricalEnterprises@Outlook.com

Published by Historical Enterprises, Santa Clara, Utah

First Edition: September 2017
Printed in the United States of America
ISBN: 978-0-9993962-0-9

The front cover image is courtesy of the Library of Congress. The handwriting on the back cover is from Abby Guy's Petition for Freedom filed in the Second Circuit Court in Hamburg, Arkansas, courtesy of University of Arkansas Little Rock Law School Library Special Collections.

Abby Guy

Race and Slavery on Trial in an 1855 Southern Court

Table of Contents

Foreword

This book is the true story of Abby Guy, a remarkable woman born into slavery, who filed a Petition for Freedom in 1855 in rural southeast Arkansas. She was audacious and undaunted by the powerful slave system she faced, and she unhesitatingly put race and slavery on trial in the courts of the state. Her story is like a thousand piece puzzle, seven hundred of which are missing, but even that much is rich with drama and intrigue, and we can reasonably fill in some of the empty spaces. Few details can be found about Abby's life except through the court documents.

Abby Guy lived in hard times. This book deals with the difficult subject of slavery and the racist society and legal system that supported it. The word "negro" in this book is never capitalized because it only appears in direct quotes from various sources, none of which in those days ever capitalized the word. People with a mixed race ancestry were in the 1850s called by the derogatory label "mulatto," meaning the offspring of a horse and a donkey. The word is used in this book because it was used then.

There exists a 76 page document that is called a "trial transcript," but a better term would be "trial record." Some portions were written in the first person, which appear as quotations in this book. Punctuation has sometimes been inserted to help the flow of reading because the original text contains extended run-on sentences. To avoid becoming bogged down in legalese, the names "Abby Guy" are inserted where the original wording says "plaintiff," and "William Daniel" for "defendant." For ease of reading, the term "cause of action" has been changed to "case." On rare occasion a word obviously missing in the original documents has been added. Other trial court documents, census records and contemporary newspapers and writings are also used. The slave laws existing at the time are frequently quoted so that the reader can have a firsthand sense of their ruthless meaning and impact of hopelessness.

The intent of this book is to tell the story of an astonishingly bold woman with an unconquerable spirit, Abby Guy.

The Statutes of Arkansas 1855

Chapter 75

Freedom

Section 1. Any person held in slavery may petition the circuit court, or judge thereof, for leave to sue as a poor person, in order to establish his right to freedom, and shall state in his petition the ground on which his claim to freedom is founded.

Chapter 1
Wrongfully Held in a State of Slavery

To the Honorable T. F. Sorrels," was the simple beginning of her story. "Your petitioners are Abby Guy and her four minor children, Elizabeth F. Daniel, Mary Daniel, John Guy, and Malissa Ann Arnold.... Your petitioners... are wrongfully held in a state of slavery, by one William Daniel.... Your petitioners state that they are not negroes or mulattoes but white persons, and are not slaves, but free."

These were the opening words of a Petition for Freedom filed on January 28, 1855, in a court in southeastern Arkansas. "The way your petitioners came to be thus wrongfully enslaved," the document explained in an almost poetic way, "is as follows. Many years ago the mother of your petitioner Abby Guy was a poor destitute orphan child in the State of Virginia, without any friends or home, and living from place to place. She was free and a white person. She was taken up by some negro traders and carried to Alabama and sold as a slave to the father of William Daniel."

Second Circuit Court Judge Theodoric F. Sorrels was accustomed to the usual run of cases coming before the courts of the state - contracts, probate issues, land disputes, criminal cases, and the other countless disagreements that torment man and cannot be settled by the people involved. Sorrels had been an attorney and a prosecutor, and was now a judge, so he had a wide range of experience. In his judicial circuit of ten counties he was the primary trial judge in the small town of Hamburg, Ashley County, Arkansas, down in the corner of the state on the Louisiana line and near Mississippi.

On that winter day in early 1855, two attorneys named John C. Waddell and Benoni S. Dubose delivered to Judge Sorrels the paperwork on a Petition for Freedom written by them for 44-year-old widow Abby Guy. The beginning lines surely got Judge Sorrel's attention. Suits for freedom were rare and usually involved black slaves who claimed they had been emancipated by their owners in a will. This case was very different. Sorrels continued to read the compelling words of the attorneys. Nothing speaks as well as the petition itself, which continued explaining the fate of Abby's mother, then of Abby and her children:

> "She [Abby's mother] found a home and remained the balance of her life with said old man Daniel and with his son Nathaniel Daniel after his death. Her condition in the hands of these two Daniels, father and son, was more favored than that of ordinary slaves, and hence she submitted to the wrong.
>
> "Your petitioner Abby was born in this period, and her condition in the hands of Nat Daniel was also more favored than that of an ordinary slave, and she submitted during his life to that condition. The two first named children above are said Nat Daniel's children. At the death of said Nat Daniel in... Alabama, some twelve or fifteen years ago, he manumitted [freed] by his last will your petitioner Abby and the children then born, to wit, Elizabeth and Mary, and also made ample provision for their support. The said William Daniel was executor of said will and assented to the manumission of your said Petitioners, and ever since until within about a month ago, has permitted your said Petitioners to enjoy perfect freedom.
>
> "Your petitioner Abby since so freed, married and had a child, and her said husband has died, and she has continued to live to herself perfectly free, till about a month ago... when said William Daniel came and took her and her said children into his possession, tore them from their home and has reduced them... to a state of slavery....
>
> "Your petitioners are by blood and inheritance free, and the manumission of them by Nat Daniel was but an admission of that previous right. Your petitioner therefore prays that Your Honor will order the issuance of the necessary writ for the purpose of trying your petitioner's rights to their freedom, and that they be permitted to sue as poor persons... and have counsel appointed, and your petitioners state that unless said William Daniel be made to give bond for the forthcoming trial and good treatment of your petitioners he will remove them beyond the

> jurisdiction of your Honorable Court, and also probably inflict on your petitioners other severities, and they therefore pray that your honor order that he give bond as required by the statute in such case, or your petitioners taken out of his hands, and your petitioners will ever pray,
>
> Abby Guy for herself and her children
> Elizabeth, Mary, John and Malissa Ann
> By B.S. Dubose & John C. Waddell"[1]

A little later Dubose filed an addition to the petition, stating that William Daniel "on the first day of December A.D. 1854... with force and arms made an assault upon the said Abby Guy and her children, and then and there, and from thence until the commencement of this suit... has kept and detained them in prison, and still so keeps and detains them, without any reasonable and proper cause whatever.... Abby and her children allege that before and at the time of the committing of the aggrievances aforesaid they were and still are free persons, and that William Daniel held and still holds them in slavery."[2] Dubose also filed another document alleging the precise offense required by the freedom statute, "trespass for false imprisonment," which had not been mentioned in the original petition.[3]

This Petition for Freedom, then, was the beginning of the fascinating story of Abby Guy, told in the now aged and yellowed pages of the trial record. As she said in the Petition, Abby wanted freedom on the basis that she and her children were "white persons, and are not slaves, but free."

Abby Guy was like everyone else. She did not choose her parents or their circumstances. She did not choose when she was born, or where, or into what type of society. She did not choose her race or ancestry. Born into slavery, she had little opportunity to move ahead in life, but she was determined to make the most of it. If she was white, or mostly white, or appeared white, she would take that condition as far as she could to make herself and her children free. Very few slaves could do this on such a basis, but for her it was a possible opening to freedom and she took advantage of it. If she had had some other avenue to freedom, she would have taken that too. She simply took what existed and did everything she could with it, and more perhaps than anyone else would have.

It seems fair to say that Abby Guy was not attempting to be the symbol of a cause. Because she was illiterate, she could not read what anti-slavery freedom advocates William Lloyd Garrison and Frederick Douglass were writing up North against slavery. She probably never heard of them. She was deep in her own overwhelming circumstances, fighting for herself and her children, doing all she could not to be pulled under by the slave system. She had no power to free anyone else; it was far from clear that she could even free herself. She was living in the moment, in the arena of a high stakes battle, and the thought that what she was doing could help anyone else besides her children probably never occurred to her. In any event, winning freedom by being white was something of no use to almost all other slaves. But anyone who could beat the slave system on any basis would be an inspiration and an encouragement to others, if she could only actually do it. It was up to her attorneys, Waddell and Dubose, to find a way, using any means they could.

In the race conscious society of the Southern states before the Civil War, there were general laws about people depending upon their racial ancestry and appearance. "Where a person... belongs to the negro race, whether of full or mixed blood, he is presumed to be a slave, that being the condition generally of such people in this State," was the law in Arkansas. "If it appears that he belongs to the white race, he is presumed to be free. If it be doubtful, whether he belongs to the white, or the negro race... it is safest to give him the benefit of the doubt."[4] The benefit of the doubt was what Abby Guy wanted, and to be declared by a court to be white and free.

There was an in-between racial group that was designated by the ugly term "mulatto." Arkansas law provided that "every person, not a full negro, who shall be one fourth or more negro, shall... be deemed a mulatto."[5] "Mulatto" was from a Spanish word for mule, a cross between a horse and donkey. "Mulattoes" were slaves and treated the same as people who were fully African.

After reading this petition, Judge Sorrels would have looked for guidance in the Statutes of Arkansas. The law provided that "any person held in slavery may petition the circuit court... for leave to sue as a poor person, in order to establish his right to freedom, and shall state in the petition the ground on which his claim to freedom is founded."[6] Abby Guy, through her attorneys, clearly stated her grounds for claiming that she was free. She was free because she was white, she said, and because even if she had been a slave, she had been set free by her owner. Her recent enslavement, then, was a dreadful, great wrong from which she should and must be released.

The next section of the law gave the judge the power and discretion to act, or not act, depending upon his own interpretation of the facts he was dealing with. "If in the opinion of the... judge the petition contains sufficient matter to authorize the commencement of a suit, the... judge shall make the following orders...."[7] This sentence made Judge Sorrels, at this moment, the gatekeeper on the freedom of Abby Guy and her children. His decision here would either shut that gate or open it to go further in the court system. If he ruled against her, that would probably be the end of the case and Abby's freedom.

Theodoric Sorrels was a rich white man who owned slaves. His decision as judge on whether there was enough information in the petition to authorize starting a lawsuit for freedom raised an important truth. To win her freedom in this lawsuit, the slave Abby Guy would need the fairness, honesty and good will of many rich white men who owned slaves. Slavery was a pervasive institution which saturated every aspect of Southern culture, and Abby would need men who would not simply do whatever was needed to protect that system. She had already obtained the help of two white men, her attorneys, Waddell and Dubose.

Judge Sorrels was only 33 years old, but had done well. He was born in Tennessee and was admitted to the bar in Mississippi in 1846. He joined a Texas regiment and fought in the Mexican War, after which he opened a law office in the small community of Princeton in Dallas County, Arkansas. In 1851 Ashley County had paid him $60 to prosecute two slaves named John and Easter for committing a crime. He had property in the Pennington Township of Bradley County, valued at about $15,000, and owned about twenty-five slaves. Would Sorrels want his own slaves gaining their freedom by filing petitions in court, or would he simply shut down that means of escape, for them and for Abby, regardless of the facts alleged by a lawyer? This case would be a test of whether he would administer justice in an even-handed manner, wherever the facts and the law led.

The petition written by Waddell and Dubose was well done and could not be treated lightly or disregarded by the Judge. It is most unfortunate that a photograph or physical description of Abby Guy does not now exist. Her attorneys simply said that she was white, and everyone knew that under the law white people could not be enslaved. Also, they said that although she had once been a slave, she had been freed by her owner. If either of those things were true, she should indeed be freed by the court. Only a corrupt judge could have found those claims did not justify a freedom suit.

But Judge Sorrels was not corrupt. He decided the petition did in fact contain sufficient facts that it should move forward to court. It was, in any event, only a preliminary decision because more information for Abby's claim would come later at a trial, and her would-be owner, William Daniel, would then be afforded the opportunity to present his version of the story. If the facts weren't really as claimed, or if she wasn't actually entitled to be free, those things would come to light in open court. For now, there were sufficient facts alleged to proceed further.

Judge Sorrels then issued the orders required by the statute. "I am satisfied that Abby Guy and her children are entitled to sue as paupers... to establish their freedom," he wrote, and ordered "that they be not removed out of the jurisdiction of the court, and that they be not subject to any severity...."[8] Severity, otherwise known as brutal violence upon powerless subjects, was, in the final analysis, the ultimate power than kept black people in slavery. Without violent enforcement, slavery would have ended long before. In this one instance, it was prohibited by law and by this order.

As required by the statute on freedom suits, Judge Sorrels also ordered that William Daniel post a $5,000 bond to guarantee that he would not remove Abby Guy and her children from the jurisdiction. That was a very large amount of money in those days. Bonds were not cash deposits but promises to obey the court order, with Daniel and other people called "sureties" promising to pay up to that amount of money if the order was violated. If Daniel failed to post such a bond with sureties, the Judge ordered that Sheriff James Norris should "take Abby Guy and her children into his possession and hire them out to the best advantage" until the case was resolved. This requirement to hire them out for labor was required in the State law and was premised upon the fact that the petitioners were held as slaves, and until their freedom was established in court their labor was not their own. Lastly, the Judge appointed Dubose and Waddell as attorneys for Abby Guy.[9]

How her attorneys were paid is not known. There are a number of possibilities of how they handled compensation for their services. Perhaps they were paid by the County. The records show that in the month of

January 1855 Dubose was paid to represent an indigent woman named Malinda Scarlett, but no entries reflect payment for representing Abby Guy. Perhaps they were paid by someone else or a group of people who supported Abby's cause. They may have done the work "pro bono," for free as a public service or as a favor to someone. It may have been that attorneys were expected to take a share of pauper cases and this was fulfilling that duty. Waddell and Dubose had asked to be appointed to represent her, and the Judge did so.

Two days later, on January 30, 1855, Dubose filed a declaration with the court. It is the only document in the lawsuit that is a statement directly from Abby Guy. She could not read or write, so it would have been written by her attorneys and she would have put her mark on it. "I, Abby Guy, do hereby consent that suit be brought in Ashley County Circuit Court for the freedom of my minor children, Elizabeth F. Daniel, Mary Daniel, John Guy, and Malissa Ann Arnold, against William Daniel in my name as next friend for said minors. Abby Guy."[10] Because her children were minors, her consent for a lawsuit was required as a technical formality.

"Consent," however, is a profound understatement. It was her emphatic insistence that her children be in this lawsuit for freedom. She was not only fighting for her own freedom, which was naturally a great motivation to do everything possible, but she was also fighting for the freedom of her children. Any parent can imagine the heartfelt desire and unstoppable will she had that her children must be free. Her younger children, eight-year-old John Guy and two or three-year-old Malissa Ann Arnold, were born free and had never known slavery. Abby's daughter Elizabeth Frances Daniel was 20 years old and nearly an adult, but this case was about gaining her freedom from enslavement and she would be in the lawsuit whether she was a minor or an adult. Mary Daniel was 16. Elizabeth and Mary had been slaves as young children.

The question of the fatherhood of the children had been partially addressed in the documents filed with the court. The story of sex between the all-powerful master and a defenseless slave is as old as slavery itself. In her Petition for Freedom, Abby Guy had fearlessly and plainly announced for the world to know that her white owner and master, the long dead Nathaniel Daniel (brother of William Daniel who now claimed he owned them) was the father of the children of his slave, Abby. No one would have been surprised at this; it was as an exceedingly common situation. It was the dirty secret of slavery that everyone knew. For all of their talk about superior and inferior races, and the wrongfulness of mixing white people and black people, white slave owners were victimizing slave women and girls on a massive and ongoing basis. White wives pretended not to know. Abby Guy had the nerve to announce in court that she had been a slave and her white owner was the father of her two oldest children, Elizabeth and Mary.

On Friday, February 2, 1855, Ashley County Sheriff James Norris served a Summons on William Daniel. The Sheriff went out to the community of Fountain Green, ten miles north of Hamburg, and served it personally on Daniel. He read the Summons to him, telling him to appear in court in April to answer the allegation of trespass by the false imprisonment of Abby Guy and her children as slaves, and to now, at this moment, post a $5,000 bond.

Daniel would not post the bond. Considering his wealth and social status, a refusal to give the bond seems more likely than an inability to do so. This turned out to a very good thing for Abby. The next day Sheriff Norris returned and collected Abby Guy and the four children and removed them from the Daniel property. It was a moment of personal triumph for Abby to have "the law" remove her from the hands of her tormenter. It was her determined intention that she would never again be under the control of William Daniel. Undoubtedly Daniel was angry as the Sheriff took Abby and the children away, and determined that they would one day be brought back to him in chains.

State law required in a freedom suit that if the owner failed to post a bond, as William Daniel now did, that "the sheriff take possession of the petitioner and hire him [in this case, Abby and her children] out to the best advantage...during the pendency of the suit."[11] The money paid for the labor would go to the county, not to the slave or the claiming owner. After all, the slave was not yet free under the law. It was not intended that the petitioner for freedom be free during the pendency of the court proceedings, but rather that slavery be continued temporarily. Although the slave would be out of the hands of the claiming owner, it would still be slavery.

On Monday, February 5th, at the front door of the courthouse in Hamburg, Sheriff Norris offered for hire the labor of Abby Guy and the children to whomever would pay the most money. That person turned out to be 70-year-old John Arnold.[12] At this point, the powerful will to be free and the determined character of Abby Guy were again made manifest. The truth is that instead of selling her labor as a slave while waiting for the trial, she and those in the community who supported her seized this moment to actually free her during that time. It would have been prearranged, involving Waddell and Dubose as well as others.

In addition to what she had said about Nathaniel Daniel being the father of her oldest two children, Abby had also announced to the world the last name of the father of her youngest child. The Petition for Freedom said that Malissa Ann's last name was Arnold, and this man John Arnold was surely her father. He was a local widower in the area, living with his son and his family. It appears that he did not own any land or slaves. The relationship between John and Abby, however, was between two consenting free adults, not between master and slave.

Arnold paid twenty five dollars for Abby's labor on the courthouse door step because he loved Abby Guy, and he took her and her children into his home for that reason. He spared her and them from being enslaved by some other higher bidder. It is not known whether anyone else made a bid on the labor, but that low price makes it seem doubtful.

When Abby and the children were seized by William Daniel back on December 1st, word would have quickly spread throughout the area. It is reasonable to believe that it was John Arnold, whose lover and child were enslaved, who decided to try to save her by going to the Hamburg law office of John C. Waddell to ask for his help. Very new to the area, having just come from Tennessee, Waddell brought into the case the longer-established attorney Benoni S. Dubose of neighboring Bradley County to help him.

Waddell and Dubose would then have informed Arnold of the state law requiring that the labor of any slave seeking freedom must be put out to the highest bidder. They then prepared to take advantage of the opportunity thus presented. Like Abby, John Arnold could neither read nor write, but he knew something about posting bonds and bidding out a female slave's labor on the front door of the courthouse. As executor of someone's will ten years earlier, he had himself done exactly that. He had the labor of a female slave sold to the highest bidder at the courthouse door in Chicot County in 1843 in the days before Ashley County was created.[13]

For the benefit of Abby and the children, Arnold made sure he was the highest bidder. He was not alone in doing this. He had to post a bond of $5,000 and have other people in the county be willing to serve as sureties, or guarantors, who promised that in the event he failed to fulfill his responsibilities under the bond they would pay any penalty for him up to that amount.

Those who were willing to serve as sureties were supporters of Abby Guy in her quest for freedom. Richard Sanders and his twin brother, Lorenzo Sanders, young men in their mid-twenties who lived only three properties away from Abby's earlier home, volunteered as sureties. So also did William Morris, an illiterate 59-year-old farmer from Beech Creek who owned land a mile and half from where Abby and her husband had lived. John Bullock, 53, a farmer living east of Hamburg, also volunteered.[14] All four sureties were within ten miles of the Guy property, and all of them owned slaves. Each one of them took a personal chance on John Arnold and on Abby Guy, pledging their property and potential liability because they believed in Abby and her cause. It was likely something their wives also supported.

So when Abby's labor was put out to bid at the courthouse front door, John Arnold was present and ready. His bond and sureties were ready. He then bid and bought, not slave labor, but temporary freedom for Abby, their daughter, Malissa Ann, and the other children, until the trial in April. Sheriff Norris released them to Arnold, and they walked away from the courthouse, surely with happy hearts.

Chapter 2
Tore Them from Their Home

Abby Guy had spent most of the previous ten years in Ashley County, Arkansas. The land she had owned was only twelve miles from Louisiana and twenty-five miles from the Mississippi River. The rural life there consisted of small farms and houses scattered throughout the countryside. "Hamburg is the county town, of about 100 inhabitants, has a fine court house, and about three stores," a newspaper article said in 1857.[15]

Ashley County was named for Senator Chester Ashley, a Little Rock lawyer and Democratic politician who was serving in the United States Senate when he was stricken ill while serving in Washington D.C. He died there in April 1848, just a few months before the creation of the county. The town of Hamburg was named, supposedly, for the large "hams" of a deer killed at that location.[16] This may have been a joke that gained circulation in the 1800s, but perhaps it is true. Another more likely story is that it was named after the city in Germany because some of the early settlers were German.

Ashley County grew rapidly. In the 1850 census, it had a population listed at 2,058. Of that number, 644 (31%) were slaves. Only five years later the population had nearly doubled to 3,500 people. Of those, about 2,250 were free whites and 1,250 (35%) were slaves. The issue now at hand was, in which category were Abby Guy and her four children? In those days and in that place, nothing else was more important than the classification that applied to them.

On December 1, 1854, Abby Guy was living as a free white person in Louisiana. She had left Arkansas and slavery behind and moved on to a new life, and had been there perhaps a year. It is unfortunate that when she left Arkansas she did not go north to a free state with her children, beyond the reach of a past slave owner. She must have felt very secure that she would be safe in a slave state. She was wrong. That was the day William Daniel had "by *force and arms*...made an *assault* upon" Abby and the children.[17] As stated in the Petition for Freedom, "William Daniel... *tore* them from their home." Daniel probably brought with him hired men who, with guns, burst in without warning, physically and forcefully kidnapped Abby and her children, put them in chains, and took them in wagons back to Arkansas to a secure place on Daniel's property from which they could not escape.

The surprise of Abby at this moment of seizure, and the tearful shock to her children, can only be imagined. Twenty-year-old Elizabeth and 16-year-old Mary, on the doorstep of adulthood, saw their intended futures shattered in an instant. The younger children, John and Malissa, who had never spent one minute of their lives as slaves, would have been bewildered and terrified. No doubt Daniel triumphantly announced to them that they were his slaves and that he was taking possession of them. Slaves had no rights, so no courts, writs or police would have been involved. This was what slave owners had a right to do.

Daniel also helped himself to all of Abby's personal property, including all the furnishings in her home, two mares and a colt, and a yoke of oxen and a cart, all of which Abby had bought with her own money.[18] To Daniel she was just a slave, and since slaves could not own property, anything she had belonged to him. Unless Abby could now win in court, he was right.

Abby Guy was angry beyond measure and determined to defeat and avenge this indignity heaped upon her and the children. In the two months from the time of their removal from Daniel's possession by the Sheriff until the trial, Abby Guy worked diligently with her attorneys to prepare her case. She wanted to be legally declared free, she wanted her children to be declared free, and she wanted her property back.

Because he lived near Hamburg, John C. Waddell would have been the attorney to work most often with Abby. Dubose's office was a day's journey away, then another day back. It was likely that it was Waddell who told her that she should fight for her freedom now, and then afterward sue for return of the property. This advice was based upon the legal principal that a slave cannot sue the master or any person for any reason except for freedom,[19] so she would need to win her freedom first, and then afterward sue for her property. The property issue, then, was dropped for the time being.

Benoni S. Dubose was a South Carolina born attorney with a law office in the small town of Warren, Arkansas. He generally did not go by his first name, but by his initials, "B.S." Today it seems odd for a lawyer to want to be known by that name, but perhaps that acronym was not used then. He was 34 years old, and it appears he did not own any slaves. John C. Waddell, formerly of Tennessee, was also 34. He and his wife had three children, and within a few years of arriving in Arkansas, owned four slaves.

One might reasonably believe that in order for William Daniel to enslave someone he had to prove that he had the legal right to do so, but that was not the case in the slave system. Because black people were always presumed to be slaves, they had to prove they were free. The burden of proof, therefore, was on Abby, not on Daniel. Dubose and Waddell had to establish and prove her right to freedom.

The slave code was relentless in its suppression of black people and the consignment of their race to lifelong servitude. "The presumption of law is that a person of African descent is a slave," was the starting rule of Arkansas society, and "in a suit for freedom, [he] must make out his title against all the world."[20] It was intended and designed to surround those of African descent with a hopeless situation. This was true in every slave state. As Abraham Lincoln said of the slave and his masters, "They have him in his prison house; they have searched his person, and left no prying instrument with him. One after another they have closed the heavy iron doors upon him, and now they have him, as it were, bolted in with a lock of a hundred keys, which can never be unlocked without the concurrence of every key; the keys in the hands of a hundred different men, and they scattered to a hundred different and distant places; and they stand musing as to what invention, in all the dominions of mind and matter, can be produced to make the impossibility of his escape more complete than it is."[21]

The attitude in this slave society was such that free speech was not allowed in Arkansas upon the subject of slavery, even for white people. "If a free person, by speaking or writing, maintains that owners have not [the] right of property in their slaves," state law provided, "he shall be confined in jail not more than one year and fined not exceeding five hundred dollars."[22]

Yet, perhaps surprisingly, in Arkansas as well as other Southern states, there was one concession to freedom. It was one slight opening in the law to those who were wrongly caught up in the system of slavery (wrongly, that is, within the context of that system). Slaves could sue for freedom if they claimed that they were mistakenly held in slavery. Abby Guy was determined to use this small window to gain freedom for herself and for her children. Only a very few people had escaped slavery by the courthouse door, but the important point was that some did escape. The legal obstacles were significant and nearly impossible to meet, just as they were intended to be.

Abby Guy was born and raised a slave, then was allowed unofficial freedom by her owner, and she lived free as a farm wife and mother. Being utterly unschooled, she would have known nothing about the statutes by the legislatures and cases by the courts concerning freedom. She just knew to the depths of her soul that she should be free, and that her children should be free, and with an iron will she pursued that freedom.

It was Abby's attorney, John C. Waddell, who would have been staying up late at night, poring over books, laws and cases, seeking a way to free her. As a recent arrival in Ashley County, it is unlikely that he knew Abby before this case. He turned out to be a man to match her will and grit; he would do everything he could. He would have looked to current laws and previous cases to help him shape his own case for Abby. Seeing how other people had succeeded or failed in similar situations would be most instructive to him on what to do now.

Abby told Waddell that her mother, who was now deceased, was a white orphan girl who had been ensnared and sold by slave traders. This meant that Abby was born to a mother wrongfully held as a slave. Waddell likely wondered if this was really true, but he accepted the word of his client. Maybe it was true. This was the starting point of his case for Abby.

Waddell would have looked first to Chapter 75 of the Arkansas Statutes, which was simply entitled "Freedom." "Any person held in slavery," it said, "may petition the circuit court... to sue as a poor person in order to establish his [her] right to freedom." If the judge found the reasons for the claim for freedom to be sufficient, then he was to "issue an order allowing the person to sue as a poor person, and assigning him counsel." Judge Sorrels had done that. Then he was to order that "the person have reasonable liberty to attend his counsel and the court, that he not be removed out of the jurisdiction of the court, and that he not be subject to any severity on account of his application for freedom." The Judge had done that as well.

Given the overall severity of the slave codes, these provisions were liberal indeed. It must be remembered, however, that they were not intended to help slaves. They were intended to help white people who had mistakenly been enslaved under the system, and black people who had been freed by emancipation and were wrongly kept in slavery. The enforcement of freedom for legally freed black people was not for the benefit of the ex-slave, but rather to enforce the right of the white owner to free them if he wanted to. It was an expression of white property rights in the slave, not of the human rights of a black person.

The Freedom statute, however, also had the proverbial mountain to climb for a slave seeking freedom. "If the plaintiff [the person seeking freedom] be a negro or mulatto, he is required to prove his right to freedom." This had an uncertain application to Abby, though, who claimed she was white and "not negro or mulatto." Nevertheless, she had been before and now was once again a slave, and she had the burden of proof. She had to show that she was white and that would prove her right to freedom. Proving the right to freedom was extremely difficult, and for almost all slaves, impossible. But if one can climb that mountain, the statute provided for the words Abby Guy wanted desperately to hear: "If the plaintiff's right to freedom is established, judgment of liberation shall be given." That was the goal.

A cruel provision in the Freedom statute was that a person claiming and winning freedom "shall not recover any damages" from the person who had illegally held her in slavery. Incredible though it may seem now, there was then no penalty to someone who had wrongfully enslaved another person.[23] Immunity had been granted to people like William Daniel. This eliminated any incentive for the would-be owner to weigh the merit of his own claim of ownership, or be fair in any way to the intended slave. If it turned out that the claiming owner was wrong, he would lose the slave but nothing else. Arkansas had this provision, but other slave states did not.

Winning freedom in court for someone in slavery could be done in only three ways. Abby had to prove she was white and therefore could not be held as a slave, that she was a slave who had been freed by a deed of emancipation from her owner, or that she was a slave who had been freed in a will when her owner died. There were no other legal roads to freedom. If she failed on these points, Abby and her children would be returned to William Daniel as slaves. Waddell and Dubose made the claims in the court documents to meet these requirements, stating in the Petition for Freedom that Abby was white and must be freed, and that, in addition, she and the oldest two children had been freed by the will of their owner.

Waddell would have been most interested in, and surely read about, a somewhat similar case from fifteen years earlier in Kentucky. It dealt with "Milly, an apparent white woman, about forty years old, who had been treated as a slave from her birth" who brought a suit for freedom against a man who held her in slavery and claimed her as his property. The similarities to Abby were obvious.

In Milly's trial, "she was exhibited before the jury for their inspection." The court held that her white color was admissible evidence that she was actually white, even though other evidence from her owner that her mother was a slave might show that, after all, she was not entitled to freedom. In Milly's case the judge refused to allow the jury to hear the information about the mother being a slave, which the Kentucky Court of Appeals said was a mistake. Milly had won the jury verdict for her freedom, but that and the resulting order of liberation were thrown out and the case sent back for a new trial.[24] Waddell learned the lesson here. He would exhibit Abby to the jury members to prove to them with their own eyes that she was white. Then, when William Daniel wanted to show that she had been born to a slave woman, Waddell would not object. He didn't want to win a jury verdict in Abby's favor only to have it be overturned later on appeal.

The harsh reality of slavery was that a child's enslavement depended on the race and status of the mother. The rule about the mother and her children was that "if she was a slave when they were born, they are slaves."[25] Abby had undeniably been born to a slave mother and had lived as a slave for the first thirty years of her life, and there was no doubt that William Daniel's attorney would show that in the trial. But that fact did not prove that her enslavement was legal, only that it had happened. Waddell likely had in his hand another case from Kentucky, which stated the obvious point that "a person held and governed as a slave, is not either physically or intellectually a free agent. It would be unreasonable, therefore, to make the fact of constrained submission, however protracted, proof that it was rightful."[26] The power to impose slavery did not make that slavery legal. This was an important legal point in Abby's favor.

It was remarkable that in slave freedom cases Arkansas law gave the right to a trial by jury. Section 6 of Article II of the Arkansas Constitution stated that "the right of trial by jury shall be inviolate." In the slave system, when all other avenues of legal rights and due process were denied, this one remnant of justice remained. It must be remembered, however, the right to a jury in a freedom suit was intended to protect not slaves, but those people who were wrongfully held as slaves.

As an experienced attorney, John C. Waddell would have known that a jury can sometimes be persuaded to go a particular way in a case no matter what the law was or what the facts were. If he could get the jury to believe in his presentation of Abby's story, the Arkansas Supreme Court on any appeal might well honor, or defer to, the jury's verdict. "Deference" to a jury decision was a long-standing tradition in American law. Waddell's legal research probably turned up another helpful freedom case where the jury had entered a verdict in favor of the slave. "We are of the opinion...," the justices held, "that the case having gone to the jury... this is not a case in which we should be justified in directing a new trial in opposition to the opinion of the jury."[27] A jury verdict for Abby Guy just might be upheld if the case was appealed.

So within the American system of justice, broken though it was on slavery and other points, was this wildcard component of the jury. The participation of the jury in a trial was then and is now part of the checks and balances within the legal system. Usually juries do the job at hand in a workmanlike manner. At its worst, the jury system empowers uninformed and inexperienced people to make important decisions. Juries can make dreadful decisions out of ignorance or prejudice. A disillusioned Mark Twain (Samuel Clemens), a contemporary of Abby Guy from the neighboring state of Missouri, would later say that "the jury system puts a ban upon intelligence and honesty and a premium upon ignorance, stupidity and perjury."[28] But at its best, the jury is a bulwark against tyranny, an escape mechanism whereby common people can do what is right no matter what the circumstances, the facts, or the law may be. That's what Waddell wanted the jury to do for Abby. The main lesson to be learned by Waddell from the freedom suits was that a very few people were actually winning their freedom. Abby Guy could be the next one to do it.

During the time between her release to John Arnold on February 5th and the trial scheduled for the first week of April, John C. Waddell and B. S. Dubose would have reviewed with Abby the facts of her life, selecting out the important matters that needed to be proven in court. Potential witnesses would have been identified, interviewed, and prepared for trial. Summonses from the Court ordering them to appear at a specific day and time would have been served upon them to insure their appearance for trial. In this case, all the witnesses in the trial would be white men.

One would expect that the first witness would be Abby herself. Putting her on the stand to tell the compelling story laid out in the Petition for Freedom would be the strongest part of her case. But it could not be so. There were two problems.

In modern times juries are permitted to hear and weigh the evidence and testimony from the people involved in the lawsuit, evaluating for themselves whether those testifying tell the truth and to what degree they do so. But there then existed a principle of law that totally prevented Abby's testimony. It was simply thought by the legal authorities of that day that a person could not honestly testify in a case where her or his own interests were at stake. "No rule of evidence is better settled than that which excludes parties from being a witness in their own suit... [A]ny immediate legal interest in the event of an action renders the interested party incompetent as a witness in that action."[29] In other words, Abby herself could not testify and would have to prove her case with the testimony of other people.

For the trial, then, the mouth of Abby Guy was closed. This is a great loss to history now, as there are no surviving direct statements from her. She would have said many things beyond what was stated in the Petition for Freedom, which would have been both intriguing and invaluable to understanding her and her life. It was a loss to her attorneys, too, who had to figure out how to make her case without her.

Abby Guy's silence was also a huge loss of information for the jury. The jury would never hear that Abby's mother was a white orphan girl without a home, going from place to place, and being captured by slave traders and sold into slavery, where she lost her freedom but found a home as a favored slave for the Daniel family. No one available as a witness would have firsthand knowledge about such things.

The jury would also not hear Abby's testimony that she and her two oldest children were set free by their master Nathaniel Daniel at the time of his death. No witness available to her could supply that information. As a result, the jury members could never hear these facts before they rendered their verdict.

There was a second legal problem with Abby Guy testifying. Under Arkansas law, a black person, even a free one, could not testify in a trial with white people. "No negro or mulatto, bond [slave] or free, shall be a competent witness in any case, except in cases in which all the parties are negroes or mulattoes."[30] William Daniel was white, and he was asserting that Abby was a slave. If true, she could not testify against him. Yet she was claiming that she was in fact white, and if she was white, then she could testify. This dilemma of logic, however, didn't have to be resolved. The rule against any party, even a white one, testifying in his or her own case saved Judge Sorrels from having to decide the matter. Abby could not testify, anyway.

In preparing the case, there was a central, unanswerable question in Abby Guy's Petition for Freedom. Even she may not have known the truth of it. Was her mother really white? It is possible, of course, that she was, and that the story was true. Or, perhaps Abby's inability to testify was just as well for her and her attorneys, as it may have eliminated the temptation or necessity of her lying under oath in open court, and her lawyers allowing her to do so. It cannot be known now with certainty, but this tale of her mother being a white orphan girl who was wrongfully enslaved was perhaps only a story, something not really true. A third possibility was that it was something her mother actually told young Abby, but whether it had underlying truth even Abby did not know.

In the Petition for Freedom, Dubose and Waddell *had* to allege that Abby had a right to be free, or else there was no case to take to court and to trial. They did their job and doubled down by claiming two independent grounds for freedom. First, they claimed that Abby was free because her mother was white and originally free, and, second, that even if she were not white Abby had been set free in the will of Nathaniel Daniel. If Waddell had said Abby's mother was a legal slave and that Abby had never been freed by her owner upon his death, Judge Sorrels would have quickly concluded that no legal case existed to go forward to court. He would have swung that gate to freedom closed after reading the petition.

In the final analysis, though, it didn't matter whether Abby Guy was actually of pure white blood or was really of mixed ancestry. What mattered was whether the jury members could be convinced to give a verdict in her favor, for whatever reason they found sufficient in their own minds. What a jury finds to be true *is* the legal truth, whether it aligns with the actual facts or not. Such thoughts would have been in the minds of Waddell and Dubose as they prepared their case.

Meanwhile, William Daniel was preparing his case for trial too. He was assembling the evidence to support his claim that Abby was in fact a slave - his slave - and that her children were therefore his slaves as well. By taking possession of them, he was only asserting a legal right he had to his property. Everyone knew this was the way slavery worked in Arkansas and in Southern society. This system of slavery was widely practiced by many people, and it was supported as an institution by many more. Such people would be on the jury.

Daniel was as determined to win the case as Abby was. He hired a top lawyer in the state of Arkansas to represent him, James Yell. It had to have been expensive to do this. His attorney was the nephew of Archibald Yell, who had been the first U.S. Congressman from Arkansas and second Governor, and who was killed while leading a regiment in the Mexican War eight years earlier. Yell County and the town of Yellville were named in honor of Archibald.

James Yell, 44 years old, was famous in his own right. At the suggestion of his Uncle Archibald, James moved his family from Tennessee to Pine Bluff, Arkansas, and opened a law office. He practiced law in trial courts all over the state and also handled appeals to the Arkansas Supreme Court. He was elected to the Arkansas Senate in 1842 and 1844, and was continually involved in politics.

Yell was also a blunt talking, forceful man who had personally gotten away with murder. The killing of Murray C. Woodworth in Yell's home town of Pine Bluff was described in a newspaper article. "It appears that Woodworth had been a candidate for Justice of the Peace...and that Yell had denounced him as a 'damn'd dog,' on hearing which Woodworth had announced his intention of stating to Yell, the first time he should meet him, what he thought of him and his conduct," reported the newspaper *Arkansas Intelligencer* in the town of Van Buren. "On the following morning, as Yell passed the tavern of Drew White, Woodworth called to him, and said he wanted to speak to him. Yell replied that he must speak quick as he was in a great hurry. Woodworth then commenced talking when Yell drew a pistol and fired it at his head, so near his face that some of the powder lodged in his cheek. By a quick movement Woodworth escaped with only a slight wound in the neck, and immediately retreated into the house. In a few moments he returned to the porch, when Yell fired a second pistol at him.... The ball flattened itself upon the hip bone, inflicting a wound which caused the death of Woodword... Mr. W was entirely unarmed.[31]

Yell was arrested at the scene of the killing but was released on bail. When the question of an indictment for murder later went before the sixteen members of the grand jury of Jefferson County, testimony was given that the night before the shooting Woodworth had made threats against Yell, and that on the morning of the incident he had told others he was going to do what he had said the previous night. The friendly grand jury found this to be justification for Yell to shoot twice and kill Woodworth, who never fired a shot and did not even have a gun. The *Arkansas Intelligencer* commented that "we do not think that there is an unprejudiced man in this community who [believes] that if Woodworth had killed Yell, under the same circumstances, he could have escaped the penitentiary for life."[32] That was probably an accurate statement. James Yell cut a wide path in Arkansas, and he walked free from this murder.

Frontier Arkansas was a rough place, and even the taint of possible murder did not slow James Yell's career. In fact, it probably enhanced it. In the 1848 presidential election, he was chosen by the Democratic Party as a presidential elector and voted for Lewis Cass in the Electoral College. Yell also became a major general in the Arkansas militia, and his legal practice continued to grow.

Now working for William Daniel, Yell began discussing the facts with his client and putting a case together. They faced the same court rule that hampered Abby Guy and her attorneys. Daniel was a party in the case and could not testify, so the case would have to be proven by the testimony of other people. The rule against parties testifying was as much a difficulty to them as to Waddell and Dubose. Daniel would have had a wealth of information about the situation, things he knew personally that he could tell the jury if permitted to do so, but his mouth was closed too.

Yell's legal case for Daniel was that Abby's mother was a mulatto and a slave, that Abby was born of a slave and had never been freed, so she was still a slave and so were her children. Extended Daniel family members who knew Abby and her mother in the old days in Alabama were summoned for trial.

Waddell and Dubose had their work cut out for them. This would be a hard fought trial. There must have been days when it seemed like this illiterate slave woman, Abby Guy, stood no chance of defeating written laws, slave masters, and powerful men, in the forum that they devised and controlled - the courtroom.

Chapter 3
The Case for Abby Guy's Freedom

The Second Circuit Court consisted of ten counties in the southeast corner of Arkansas,[33] and at the end of March 1855 the traveling legal show of the Judge and the lawyers arrived in Hamburg. "A judicial circuit at that early day was an immense domain, over which the bench and bar regularly made semi-annual trips," wrote an 1890 history of the state. "The court was literally 'in the saddle.' The saddle bags were their law offices.... Circumstances thus made the bench and bar as social a set as ever came together."[34]

The description of Abraham Lincoln's law practice at that same time up in Illinois applied here: "Lawyers and court officials traveled together from one county seat to another for sessions of the circuit court, moving by atrocious frontier roads and stopping in inns, taverns and boarding houses where accommodation was not always of the best."[35] In Hamburg there were no hotels, and visitors would have to find places to stay overnight in the homes and outbuildings of the nearby people, or in tents or wagons. Sheriff Norris was instructed by the County Court to reserve two of the rooms on the main floor of the courthouse, presumably for Judge Sorrels to occupy.

In remote rural areas with little diversion from everyday work life, the arrival of the judge and lawyers provided a popular public diversion. There were new people in town to talk to and new issues to talk about. People would attend court to see what was going on in the community and to listen to the oratory of the lawyers. "In those days," says one history, "lawyers became rich and famous by courtroom advocacy, in part because trials were public entertainment that eased the monotony of daily life, especially in rural areas, where entertainment options were limited."[36]

The two storey courthouse in Hamburg was made of home produced timber. It was about forty feet square and had a roof sloping from an apex to the four directions, with a flag pole extending up from the center. It had a court room upstairs and four offices down. It was heated by a chimney made of home baked brick.[37] The Ashley County Court, which was something different from the Circuit Court and functioned like a County Commission, was still trying to figure out how to pay for the building. In January 1855 it issued an order that all the justices of the peace meet "for the purpose of devising a means of paying for the court house." When they met on April 16th they imposed a property tax and a poll tax to pay the expense of the new building.[38]

The April 1855 term of the Second Circuit Court in Hamburg was busy. All legal matters arising in the last six months had been saved for handling at this time. The Judge gaveled the Court into session, and various cases were heard over several days.

Wednesday, April 4, 1855, was the day set for the trial of Abby Guy's freedom. It was a momentous day at the courthouse in Hamburg, Arkansas. It may have been the first jury trial held in the new courthouse. There was no newspaper in Ashley County at that time, so there is no description of events that might have been covered by a local reporter or editor. No surviving newspapers from other cities in Arkansas mentioned it, and probably none did.

Judge Theodoric F. Sorrels, who had been elected to his first term as judge only the prior August, was in charge. His authority to be sitting as a judge at all had been challenged by the Arkansas Attorney General over the interpretation of a technical election law, which had just recently been resolved by the State Supreme Court in Sorrels' favor.[39]

Judges often consider themselves the center of the universe when a trial is held, and they have a way of making their status and power known to the attorneys, the parties, the witnesses and the audience. Their personalities are continually on display in court, and their strengths are required to keep rambunctious lawyers under control. Sorrels was no exception. "He is what the world calls eccentric," a contemporary writer said of him, "stern and austere...." He had an unusually distinctive signature. A lifelong Methodist, he was "quaint, honest, sincere, religious, he makes no compromise with vice."[40] He would need to be strong to deal with James Yell.

Of course, Abby Guy was present in the courtroom. Her daughters, Elizabeth, Mary and Malissa Ann, and her son, John, were there as parties in the lawsuit. Doubtless, John Arnold was in the first public row behind Abby, and surely other supporters as well, perhaps including the men who had been sureties for Arnold's bond and her women friends who wanted her to regain her freedom. The nature of the case was such that it had to have caused a widespread interest, maybe even a sensation, in the community. People knew her, they knew William Daniel, and they knew about slavery. It had all the elements of an exciting trial. It seems likely that the courtroom was overflowing with curious onlookers that day.

Abby's attorneys, John C. Waddell and Benoni S. Dubose, were there. They had seven witnesses on hand, waiting around the courthouse and grounds until it was their turn to testify. William Daniel was present along with his attorney, James Yell. They had five witnesses standing by. The fact that Daniel was in the position of having to legally enforce his ownership of an upstart slave woman was something that likely stirred concern among other slave owners, some of whom may have been present to show their support. A verdict for Daniel would preserve the status quo and their own power over their slaves.

The Jury

There would be no jury of her peers for Abby Guy. In those days, women neither voted nor served on juries. It goes without saying that slaves also did not sit on juries. The female slave Abby would have to win her case by convincing twelve free white men that she should be free too. That was a daunting requirement. Abby Guy and William Daniel each had reason to believe that people in the community would be supportive of her or his respective position, and that this would be reflected in the jury. Daniel likely felt that a jury of men, some of whom would themselves be slaveholders, would be friendly to his claim of ownership of a slave woman. But Waddell and Dubose were counting on another factor in the courthouse that day, that those men would be attracted to, intrigued by, and sympathetic to, Abby Guy and her claim for freedom.

Eighteen men from around Ashley County had been summoned to appear, from whom a jury of twelve would be selected for the trial. The law was that "every... juror shall be a free white male... above the age of twenty-one years." The court clerk would write the eighteen names on pieces of paper, then draw out twelve to be the jury members "if they stand indifferent between the parties." If one had something that made him favor one party or the other, that person would be dismissed and another name drawn for the jury. The pay for one day's jury duty was one dollar.[41]

Jurors are inherently interesting group. Often times they act predictably based upon their backgrounds, professions and circumstances. Yet other times they act unpredictably, demonstrating an independence or objectivity that varies from what may be expected. They can act intelligently, nobly, and in response to the actual facts, or they can act ignorantly, not caring what the truth is, and not ever understanding what the case was even about. Lawyers want to know everything they can about each juror - age, occupation, marital status, whether they owned slaves, and any other information they can learn about them. Attorneys try to prepare presentations and closing arguments that will appeal to the perceived characteristics of the jurors. It's a chancy thing, but there is a skill to it.

The predominant factor in this case was slavery, and so the most important thing to know about a juror was whether he owned slaves himself. It was a certainty that many of the jurors would. It might then be expected that in this case they would act in their own interest by preserving and protecting slavery, which was what Yell and Daniel hoped for. Unmotivated slave-owning jurors were going to find for Daniel. On the other hand, the fact that someone did not own slaves did not necessarily mean that a juror was against slavery. Perhaps he in fact did not like slavery, but it was also possible that he was poor and could not afford slaves, or that he was young and had not yet earned enough to buy them.

Yet people can sometimes detach themselves from their own interests and see and act fairly, and that was what Waddell and Dubose worked toward. They had to give the jurors a reason and a way to rule for Abby Guy. The reason would be to do justice to this woman and her children; the way was to simply find that she was white. This basis might be non-threatening to, and acceptable to, slave-owning jurors because their own slaves, after all, were not white.

So it was, then, that Waddell, Dubose and Yell would have looked with the greatest interest at the group of men from which a jury would be selected. Once they were known, the parties, supporting witnesses and friends would have informed the attorneys what they knew about each one.

The eighteen men were a cross section of local free white men over twenty-one years old. A typical man in Ashley County, Arkansas, in 1855 was a farmer who was married, had several children, worked his own land, and owned a few slaves. That list described seven of the potential jurors, namely, Ambrose Bull, age 48, John C. Downey, 47, Jefferson B. Pippen, 34,

Cecilius J. Hundley, 34, Matthew G. Pardue, 44, William Morris, 59, and Joseph P. Dean, 34. John Wallace, 39, was in this mold but had no children. Robert White, 45, and James W. Lacy, 34, were farmers but had no slaves. The prospective juror William Morris was one of the sureties for the bond posted by John Arnold when he hired the labor of Abby Guy, which likely indicated that he supported Abby. The record does not indicate an objection to his service on the jury based upon this fact. Perhaps he was not one of the twelve selected and so it did not matter.

Jurors Lemuel Denson, 26, and Robert Withers, 34, were carpenters. Denson was married and Withers was single. Neither owned slaves. G. J. Williams, 33, was a merchant in the town of El Dorado and owned no slaves. A. J. Riley, 29, was a married farm laborer who owned no land or slaves. Other men on the jury panel were James Duncan, J. A. Thomas, Wash Miller, and William Cockerham, about whom nothing is known.[42]

Except for William Morris, all of the potential jurors could read and write. Every one of these men was Southern born and raised. Not one of them came from a free state, and all had known slavery as a way of life their entire lives.

The record shows that "Ambrose Bull and eleven others, good and lawful men of the County of Ashley, who, being duly sworn and impaneled, were sworn well and truly to try the issues joined in this case, and a true verdict render according to the evidence."[43] After the foreman Ambrose Bull, it is not known which eleven of the other seventeen men actually served on the jury. Six were not selected and were released from jury duty.

It is too much to expect that these twelve men knew nothing of the case and the people involved. In rural areas with a small population like Ashley County people often knew each other, or at least knew about each other. William Daniel was a prominent owner of land and slaves who lived in Fountain Hill. Abby Guy was known by many living on the bayou on the east end of the county. The people standing by to be witnesses would be known, or known of, by some or many of the jurors. Perhaps a few jurors from more distant areas of the county came with a blank slate of information; others had existing knowledge or at least the rumor of it. There is no reason to doubt that the chosen jury members each honestly intended to honor his oath to follow the evidence that would be presented in the coming trial, and to render a true verdict based on that evidence.

"The parties all being ready for trial, this case came on to be tried," recited the court record.[44] The packed courtroom would have been tense with anticipation. The judge would have been at a desk with his back to a wall or window, facing the two tables of the parties where the attorneys and clients sat, and the public sitting in the seats beyond. The twelve jurors would be in the front but off to one side, with a witness chair somewhere between the jury and the judge. The witnesses would have been outside the courtroom, waiting to be called in one at a time to testify.

Richard Stanley

Judge Sorrels called for Waddell and Dubose to present the case for the freedom of Abby Guy and her children. They had the burden of proof in the trial so they went first. They called their opening witness, Richard Stanley. It is reasonable to interpret that every witness for Abby personally supported her claim for freedom. An unsupportive witness always has ways to make his testimony undesirable to a party, so an attorney would not call an unwilling witness if others are available to cover the same information. Nevertheless, it would be expected that in his testimony, each witness would be essentially honest in answering all questions. As it turned out, they were honest, and witness truthfulness was never an issue in the trial.

Richard Stanley was about 45 years old, a married man with three children. His wife, Martha, was 35 years old and probably a friend of Abby. He lived on and worked the farm owned by his 90-year-old father, Shadrack, and his 80-year-old mother, Rachel.[45] They lived less than a mile from the land where Abby Guy had once lived.[46] They did not own any slaves.

His testimony was fairly short but strong in content for establishing the fundamental case for freedom. Taking the stand, Stanley would have been led by the attorneys Waddell or Dubose through his testimony on a question and answer basis. The existing trial record states the testimony as if it were a narrative or a long statement, but it would have instead been presented through short answers to short questions. All of the witnesses would have given their testimony in a question and answer format.

Stanley testified that he knew Abby Guy and the children when they were "living on... Bayou Bartholomew."[47] Abby lived next to the longest bayou in the world, a 350 mile long waterway with adjacent swamp land called Bayou Bartholomew. It meandered through Arkansas and Louisiana, providing rich soil and abundant and varied wildlife.

"She was working for herself," Stanley continued, "and making a support working and selling her own crop."[48] Waddell and Dubose were establishing an important point through Stanley's testimony, that Abby did not live like a slave. Rather, she lived her life as a free person, supporting herself by running a farm. Although not mentioned in the trial record, Stanley might have mentioned, as shown in the 1850 census, that Abby also worked as a "spinstress," earning cash with cloth, needle and thread.[49]

The testimony of all the witnesses took place long ago, within a slave-based society and legal system which no longer exists. The words of the witnesses in this trial had their plain meaning, but they also had unspoken implications, a coded message, understood in that time and place by the members of the jury. Slaves didn't run farms and sell their own crops; they were not allowed to do such things and did not have the freedom to do them. It was believed in that era that blacks were not intelligent enough to do them, and that only free white people did and could do those things. Since Abby ran a farm and sold a crop, the inevitable conclusion was that she must be white.

Then Waddell moved the focus from what Abby did to support herself to how she was accepted in society by white people. Abby and her children "passed as free persons," Stanley said. "The oldest girl boarded out and went to school on Beech Creek. They lived eight or nine years on the Bayou and visited among white folks, went to church parties, etc." From this testimony, the jury could see that Abby Guy was fully a part of white society. Slaves didn't pass as free persons, and slave girls were not boarded out to school or educated in any way. Raised as a slave, Abby herself was illiterate but she was making sure her children could read and write, something she could not teach them. The 1850 census taker, probably light heartedly from a discussion with Abby, listed the occupation of the then 16-year-old Elizabeth Frances as the "Belle of Hamburg Dance." It isn't certain what that meant, but it doesn't sound very much like slavery. The fundamental implication of Stanley's testimony was that Abby and the children were free white persons, and they were accepted as such. The children were certainly being raised as free people, and they were parties in this suit along with their mother. Since Abby had been free for nearly ten years, the younger two children had never been slaves at any time. Was the jury going to make them slaves now? Waddell was moving them toward a conclusion that this would be a horrific thing for them to do, and that they had the power to prevent it.

Then Waddell got from the witness the precise statement he most wanted. Richard Stanley simply said, *"I should suppose they are white."* This statement directly said the very thing that Abby and the lawyers wanted the jury to find to be true in their verdict, that Abby and the children "are white." Once the jury found that to be the truth, they would all be free.

Stanley went on to say that Abby "lived part of the time openly with a man named Guy, and Abby passed as Mrs. Guy." He stated, though, that he did not personally know if she was actually married to him.[50] This was another important point. It was unstated in the record, but everyone in the courtroom that day knew that in Arkansas law "all marriages of white persons with negroes or mulattoes are declared to be illegal and void."[51] Abby "passed" as married to a white man, so then she must be white.

James Guy, Abby's husband, was doing his best to live the American dream of owning land and building a farm and life on the frontier. He had settled in the Bayou Bartholomew country before 1840. The census that year recorded him as a single white man in his forties, employed in agriculture, living alone, and owning no slaves.[52] In 1846 the United States granted him ownership of the sixty-three acre parcel he had hacked out of the wilderness just west of and adjacent to the bayou.[53] That land is located on the west side of the bayou northwest of the modern community of Parkdale, Arkansas.

After arriving in Arkansas as a slave in 1844, Abby was a year later living with James Guy as a free woman. This was extremely audacious for her to do. She knew she had been a slave in Alabama, and to now live as the wife of a white man in a slave state was a daring public announcement of freedom. She defied her past owner, William Daniel, and anyone else to do something about it. No one did.

James Guy obviously did not care about Abby's prior life. He took her for what and who she was, and openly embraced her before the world. He gave her his last name, something she had not had before. The Petition for Freedom recited that Abby was married, implying that they were actually married in a legal ceremony, but no surviving records substantiate that. The circumstances of their living together, presenting themselves to others as being husband and wife, and having children together, could have given rise to a common law marriage, but Arkansas has never recognized such unions. Even so, common law relationships, whether a legal marriage or not, were an everyday situation, especially on the frontier.

William Daniel never made a claim on Abby as long as James Guy was alive. When Daniel first heard that she had moved in with Guy, he did nothing about it. Surely the thought crossed his mind of whether he should claim her, but he decided to let it go. He may have been content with Abby living as a free person, or he may not have wanted to tangle with James Guy.

James and Abby Guy had two children. Their son John was born in 1846, and daughter Delphia in 1850. James was the step-father to Elizabeth Frances and to Mary, who took the last name of Guy as their own. That was their last name in the 1850 census. Unfortunately, their time together as a family was short. For reasons not known, James, still in his fifties, died in 1849 while Abby was pregnant. Abby became a 38-year-old widow with four children. Their baby Delphia was born a few months afterward, and she in turn died sometime prior to 1855.[54] Malissa Ann Arnold was born perhaps in 1852 or 1853, two or three years after James Guy's death.

Richard Stanley continued his testimony before the jury. Several years ago, he said, the widow Abby Guy asked him to move her and her family, for which she would pay him. What he did not say at this point, but which was understood by all who were present, was that this situation had slave law implications. Slaves could not make business contracts such as the one being proposed by Abby. Also, white people could not deal with a slave, such as moving someone or being hired to do something for pay, without the consent of the slave's owner. Arkansas statutes provided that if any person dealt with a slave without the consent of the owner, the white person must pay $10 to the master and $20 to the county.[55]

Stanley had heard something in the bayou back country talk that gave him pause, that William Daniel over in Fountain Hill had owned Abby Guy as a slave. Knowing this owner consent rule of slave society, he did not want to get into any trouble with the law so he handled it in an aboveboard manner. He went directly to Daniel and told him of Abby's request to move her. "I asked William Daniel if I could do so," Stanley said. "He told me that he had nothing to do with her. I asked him who would pay me for it. He said Abby could pay me."[56]

This was a damaging admission by William Daniel. He went beyond simply giving consent for Stanley to move Abby, but said that Abby could make her own contract and pay for it herself. Under the law, only white people could do such things. Even more importantly, Daniel repudiated that he was the owner of Abby at all, saying that he had nothing to do with her. What Daniel was really saying, in the final analysis, was that Abby Guy was free and he did not then own her or claim her as a slave.

Such an admission as this, that Daniel did not claim Abby as a slave when specifically asked if she was one and whether he was the owner, was something for the jury to seriously consider in this suit for freedom. Though the statement itself did not actually set her free legally, it was certainly good evidence that Daniel considered her free at the time he said it. Yell could try to overcome it or explain it away, but it was damaging to Daniel's claim now.[57]

In this manner and by this witness, Richard Stanley, attorneys John C. Waddell and Benoni S. Dubose had laid out the foundation of the case for the freedom of Abby Guy. She was white, and thought to be white by white people, and specifically considered to be so by this white witness. She was accepted by local white society. She acted as a free person, living openly as the wife of a white man, and then after his death supporting herself on the farm by raising crops as free people do. William Daniel, the man who now claimed to own her, had said he had nothing to do with her, and that she could do such slave-prohibited things as living where she wanted, and enter into contracts with white people. When given the opportunity to say that he owned her, he said that he had "nothing to do with her." Richard Stanley had gotten things off to an excellent start for Abby's case for freedom.

The Physical Display of Abby Guy and the Children

Southern slave law held that "a white person of unmixed blood can not be a slave; but one [that is] apparently white may have a taint of African blood and be a slave.... A jury... must consider the whole evidence."[58] The point of the trial was to prove that Abby and the children were white, so the "whole evidence" included what they actually looked like in their physical features. Waddell and Dubose, then, moved to have the jury members closely look at and observe Abby and each of the four children. In other words, they were to be stand before, and be physically displayed to, the twelve men of the jury for their close and personal inspection of the plaintiffs' racial features.

William Daniel's attorney, James Yell, strenuously objected. His objection may have been on the basis that it violated the rule against parties testifying for themselves. Here, it could be argued, the plaintiffs were testifying with their bodies if not with their words.

There was also an undeniable sexual undertone which necessarily arises in such a situation, with men instructed to carefully look over a woman to observe closely her physical characteristics. Perhaps Abby's features and attractiveness were something that men would consider to be a strong point for Abby. Two of the daughters, Elizabeth and Mary, were 20 and 16 years old, and they, too, were displayed. It can be understood that the defense wanted to prevent this from happening.

This process could be seen as demeaning in nature and personally humiliating, but that probably was not the way Abby saw it. More than demeaning, it was necessary, and Abby Guy was willing to do whatever was necessary to win her freedom. She had a bold character, a strong will to succeed, and a confidence in herself. She was determined to be free, and this lookover by the gentlemen of the jury was an opportunity to get them on her side. Her attorneys must have believed that this display would be highly influential in winning the case, or they would not have asked the judge to permit it.

It is most unfortunate that no detailed physical description or photograph of Abby exists. It must be concluded here that in appearance she was racially white in her personal features. Logic demands this conclusion because if it were not so, this courtroom tactic would clearly have backfired, and she and her attorneys would not have sought this display. This is not a situation where there would be any overlooking of, or winking at, physical characteristics considered to be consistent with slaves. It would have been suicidal to the case to have her show the jury members that she had features which could be deemed remotely African in nature, and which would have condemned her to slavery.

Another objection raised by Daniel's attorney, James Yell, would have been that the jury would not know the importance of what they were seeing as they looked at Abby and the children. How would an ordinary person from the back country of southeast Arkansas know the subtle physical nuances of actual racial ancestry? An expert in human racial features would be necessary to explain to the jury what physical characteristics meant in terms of identifying race.

Lastly, Yell probably objected because he knew that this was a strong point for Abby Guy, and he did not want the jury to focus on that strong point. Rather, he wanted the jury to focus on the slave documents he was going to introduce later. Objecting to the best evidence of the other side is what lawyers do. They are not seeking justice or what is right under the circumstances, they are representing the interests of their clients, whether those be right or wrong.

The law was on the side of Waddell and Dubose on this point. The Kentucky case of the slave woman named Milly, mentioned previously, supported such an exhibition to a jury.[59] Another Kentucky case gave helpful instruction for Judge Sorrels to utilize in this case now. When the physical display is made, it said, "the jury [members] are to make their own deductions from the inspection; the judge should not decide upon the color and instruct" the jury what it is. The court in that case went on to state an obvious point: "The highest and best evidence that can be given... to a jury is the evidence of... their senses, as where, in a suit involving the freedom or slavery of a party, he stands identified before a jury. They can have no better evidence of his color."[60]

Judge Sorrels followed the course set in these cases and overruled Yell's objections. After all, this was a trial about a person's race, and that determination could not be accomplished without the jury members actually looking at Abby and the children, awkward and embarrassing though that may have been to both the parties and the jurors. He simply told the jury members to apply their own knowledge and experience about the races and to await any upcoming expert testimony.

"Here the plaintiffs were personally presented in Court," the trial record notes, "and the judge informed the jury that they had the right, and should treat their observation and inspection of plaintiffs' persons as evidence; and might and should apply, in the observation of their persons, their knowledge of the distinction between the negro and the white races." The Judge also told them, if expert witnesses on race were called later in the trial, to also apply "such rules as might be proven to them to be reliable means of determining the existence of negro descent or negro blood."[61]

And so Abby and the children stood before the jury members for their close inspection.

William M. Ducker

The next witness called by Waddell and Dubose was William M. Ducker. He was a brilliant choice for a witness. As the first sheriff of Ashley County after it was created, Ducker was known to all, had experience with almost everyone in that frontier rural area, and would have carried a great deal of personal influence with the men of the jury. He was not a stranger to them. His simple act of testifying as part of the Abby Guy presentation sent a strong message to the jury of his support for her.

Ducker was 40 years old, a slave owner, and lived southwest of Fountain Hill only a couple of miles from William Daniel. Daniel could not have been happy with Ducker being a part of Abby's case.

Sheriff Ducker's testimony was not about law enforcement. He was also the "ex-officio assessor and collector of taxes for Ashley County,"[62] and this was the subject of the questions directed to him. His testimony was about his assessment duties and whether William Daniel listed Abby Guy as slave property for taxation purposes. This was valuable information. Daniel had a legal duty to list his slave property, and any failure to do so would be an admission by him that he did not claim ownership of Abby.

William M. Ducker testified that he or his deputy assessed the property of William Daniel every year. "I took the assessment of his property two or three years myself. In listing his property he put his slaves in families and did not list them by name. I can not say that Abby Guy was listed by him or not. Daniel swore to the list.... Daniel in listing his negroes would name the head of the family and make a gross estimate of their value. Abby was never listed or named on such occasions, so far as I know."[63]

Although stated somewhat ambiguously, this testimony demonstrated that William Daniel in years past had not claimed Abby and her children as his slaves. When he named the head of the slave family, he never listed Abby. No one else would have been the head of her slave family - certainly not the free white man James Guy. After Guy's death she herself was not listed as the head of the family, and she lived with no one else, so Daniel clearly had not claimed her or her children as slaves.

It was not stated in the trial record, but it was probably mentioned in his testimony that Sheriff Ducker was the census taker for Ashley County five years earlier in 1850. In fulfilling that job he went to the homes of both William Daniel at Fountain Hill and Abby Guy down on Bayou Bartholomew. On October 22, 1850, Daniel listed his slaves for Ducker's records. He owned fifteen, who were not listed by name but were stated by age, sex and race (meaning "black" or "mulatto"). Daniel did not list a 39 year old "mulatto" woman, and he did not list any children corresponding to the ages of Elizabeth, Mary, John or Delphia. He had, beyond dispute, not claimed at that time that Abby and her children were his slaves.[64] This was important information for the jury.

Then the Sheriff's testimony turned to personal matters. "Abby was living with Guy when I moved to the state, and when I lived on the bayou," he said. "I have seen them visiting."[65] These words confirmed for the jury what Richard Stanley had said. It was known that James Guy was a white man. Ducker had seen James and Abby Guy visiting among white people, and here he was now saying that Abby was accepted and not rejected by white society. In a slave state an interracial couple would not have been socially acceptable, and any marriage would have been illegal.

"Guy at his death gave her a piece of land," Ducker said. "It was listed for taxation one year. I do not know that Abby paid the tax on it that year. I as Public Administrator took charge of Guy's estate."[66] This was another statement with unspoken but clear implications. Slaves could not own land because everything they had belonged to their owner. Since Abby Guy owned land, then she was treated as white so she must be white. When Sheriff Ducker went to Abby Guy's house as the 1850 census taker, he listed Abby Guy as owning 40 acres of land that had a value of $250.

The discussion turned to taxing the personal property of Abby Guy. Ducker said that "I never thought of taxing them as the law exempted widows, and I passed them without inquiry." Here again, the implication was more important than the words themselves. Poor white women who were widows were by state law not to pay property taxes. The Sheriff not only passed over Abby but did so "without inquiry," meaning there was no doubt in his mind that she was white and that she was accepted as white, and this tax exemption applied to her.

As attorneys do, Daniel's attorney, James Yell, tried to get a concession from Ducker on cross-examination. Yell wanted to extract an admission that in some way took back or minimized what the witness had just said, and he partially succeeded. Ducker agreed that slaves were not listed for taxation by name, meaning that the absence of Abby's name was not necessarily meaningful. The Sheriff held firm on the essential point, though, and took it even further by saying, "I don't know that Abby was ever William Daniel's slave."[67]

As much by his presence on her side as by his testimony, Sheriff Ducker had been a strong witness for Abby.

What William Ducker actually thought of Abby Guy's racial ancestry may not have been stated in the trial. It may have been revealed, though, in the census record he made when he came to her door on November 20, 1850. By federal law, the oath of office for census takers that year was that "I do solemnly swear that I will, to the best of my ability, enumerate... all the inhabitants... and will collect... the other statistical information... and faithfully perform all the duties enjoined on me." This means that the record he created that day should have been accurate.

On those census records, at the top of the page, it stated that this was a listing of the "free inhabitants in Union Township." Ducker listed Abby and the children on the free inhabitants page, and not on the separate document called "slave inhabitants," so he definitely considered her to be free.

On the line for each person listed in the census there were columns in which to put information about that person. After the individual's name, the recorder was to state in separate columns that person's age, sex, and "Color (White, black, or mulatto)." The instructions given to all census takers, subject to the oath each had taken, was that, "Under heading 6, entitled 'Color,' in all cases where the person is white, leave the space blank; in all cases where the person is black, insert the letter B, if mulatto, insert M. *It is very desirable that these particulars be carefully regarded.*"[68] Here was another emphasis on the importance of accuracy in the racial designation in the census, and the duty of the census taker to get it right.

For Abby Guy, the Sheriff put down 39 for age, F for sex, and M for color. "Mulatto." He also put down M for each of the children, Elizabeth Frances, Mary, John and Delphia. He had designated each and all of them as "mulattoes."

Why did he do this? Ducker's designation of Abby and the children as "mulatto" had been made four years before this lawsuit and its controversy, so it would seem to have the credential of an honest assessment. "Mulatto" may or may not have been the true opinion of

William Ducker. Just like the first witness, Richard Stanley, the Sheriff beyond doubt heard that William Daniel had a claim on Abby, and, with this information in the back of his mind, it may been the reason he wrote down "M." Or, perhaps it really was what he thought or observed, that they were "mulatto." But if he had observed that she and the children were of mixed race, then the jury members would have observed it, too, when they were displayed to the jury members. Waddell would never have had his clients submit to close inspection because the case would have then been lost. Whatever the explanation, James Yell would have been pleased to have known that information to impeach Ducker on cross examination. But the census records had been turned over to the federal government years before.

Ducker's inner thoughts can never be known now. What is known is that at this trial on April 4, 1855, William Ducker testified for Abby Guy. It is reasonable to believe that he wanted her and the children to be free.

Jeremiah Oats

The next witness was Jeremiah Oats. He was a 55-year-old farmer with a wife and four children, who lived not many miles from where Abby had lived with James Guy. His wife, Mary, was the same age as Abby, and they probably were friends. It appears that Oats did not own any slaves.

"When I first came to Arkansas, Abby wanted me to haul some cotton for her," Oats testified. "I did so. A year after she wanted me to move a fence." These simple transactions illustrated again that Abby was living and acting like a free white person. They also invoked the same laws about dealing with slaves that had troubled the earlier witness, Richard Stanley. It was illegal for white people to deal with a slave without the consent of the owner.

By the time of the second transaction Oats had heard something about Abby. "I had before heard that William Daniel had control of her," he continued. Oats did the same thing as Stanley. To avoid getting in any kind of trouble, he went directly to William Daniel and asked him about the situation. He got the same response as Stanley. "I saw him and asked him about my doing the work for her, and who would pay me for it if I did. He said he had nothing to do with it." Again Daniel failed to assert ownership of Abby when specifically asked. For the second time, Daniel's own words were weighing in Abby's favor.

At this point, however, the conversation of Oats with Daniel about Abby Guy took a deeper turn, more to the point of the trial. "I told him they called her a negro," he said to Daniel in something of a challenge. "Daniel said they could not prove it," Oats went on. "He said she can make her own contracts and pay her own debts out of her property, and that I could deal with her as I pleased."[69]

Here was an outright admission by William Daniel that no one could prove that Abby was of African descent, which was of vast importance to Abby's case and detrimental to Daniel's. The meaning for the jury, then, was that she was white. She could act as any free person, making contracts, paying debts and owning property. None of it involved Daniel, and he was not making any ownership claim or even claiming that she was of black ancestry. H was acknowledging that Abby could own property.

By calling Jeremiah Oats as a witness, Waddell and Dubose had solidified their case for Abby Guy. Oats reinforced everything that Richard Stanley had said, plus added the important admission from William Daniel that no one could prove Abby Guy was black. This was a refutation of the testimony that they knew was coming from Daniel's witnesses about Abby being a slave. Oats was dismissed as a witness.

Keightly Sanders

It can be safely said that the Sanders family was on the side of Abby Guy. Her neighbors, the brothers Richard and Lorenzo Sanders, had pledged themselves as sureties for John Arnold so that he could free Abby by successfully bidding on her labor during the time before the lawsuit. Now their uncle Keightly Sanders was called to testify for her as a witness.

Keightly had been born in South Carolina in 1792, so he was now 62 years old. He claimed to be a veteran of the War of 1812 and was known to like his liquor. Sanders had a wife and two daughters still at home on a farm in White Township, which was where William Daniel's home was also located. In an Ashley County history it was said that Keightly "was locally known as quite a character. He walked everywhere he went unless, of course, it was necessary to haul something.... He had a gait of his own and had an expression, 'Lord God, honey,' which prefaced most of his conversation. He also had the idiosyncrasy of... staring at the one with whom he talked. He was a man of property and owned several slaves which he mortgaged when necessary to get local credit...." In 1850 Sanders owned four slaves, apparently a 48-year-old woman and her three children, aged 20, 16 and 14. He lived only two properties away from the jury foreman, Ambrose Bull.

"His vocabulary was made up largely of curse words which flowed in his conversation like water from a spring," the history continued, but he had an optimistic streak because "he never accepted anything as the worst."[70] When his brother died in 1849, Keightly didn't accept that as the worst, and became the guardian of his brother's twin sons, Richard and Lorenzo, and their sister, Lydia. A lifelong Southerner and slave owner, he was also optimistic for Abby Guy.

Taking the stand, Sanders said he had "talked a great deal with William Daniel about Abby, but never heard him say she has no negro blood in her. It was understood that Daniel had title papers to her. I heard him say so." Making it known now that there were slave documents on Abby was a wise approach by Waddell. He knew that Yell was going to put on a defense claiming Abby was a Daniel slave since birth and that he had the documents to prove it. Dealing with it preemptively in the middle of Abby's own case perhaps would defuse any surprise and some of the adverse impact the papers would have later when brought out by Yell. This tactic also implied that those documents were not all that important.

Then Sanders discussed Abby's life as a free woman. "When she lived on the bayou she managed her business as a free woman, and visited among the whites as an equal. William Daniel came to Arkansas in 1844, and from that time until just before the institution of this suit Abby and the children had lived to themselves as free in this state, except for a year or two past they moved to and lived in Louisiana."[71]

Waddell and Dubose had, through these witnesses, now proven to the jury beyond all doubt that Abby Guy and her children had been living as free white people for ten years. Stanley, Ducker, Oats and Sanders had each sworn to it. It was something not even William Daniel and James Yell could deny, and would not even try to deny. They could only try to explain it away.

Sanders was dismissed from the stand.

A. Bull

Historical records do not tell everything, nor do they present enough information to allow one to explain or understand all that happened in the Abby Guy trial. One inexplicable occurrence was the testimony of the next witness called by Waddell and Dubose in the trial, named in the trial record as "A. Bull." Ambrose Bull was twice stated in the trial record to be the foreman of the jury, but then there was the testimony of this person called "A. Bull."[72] There were two men by that name in Ashley County at that time: Ambrose Bull, 48, who has been previously described, and his nephew, Ambrose Bull, 24. The nature of the testimony from the witness A. Bull about events in 1849 would seem to indicate the witness was the uncle because the nephew would have only been 19 at that time.

Impartial juries, in both criminal and civil cases, are a bedrock of the American justice system. That was as true in 1855 as it is today. No witness should be allowed to be a juror, and no juror should be allowed to be a witness. No juror should be the nephew or uncle of a key witness for one of the parties.

However, when this witness was called, no objection was noted in the record, and James Yell would certainly have made a strong one had something been amiss. Whatever the circumstances actually were must have been acceptable at the time to the attorneys on both sides and to the judge. Perhaps a mistake was made in the trial record when the name of the witness was written down, and his real name was actually something else altogether.

Whoever he was - A. Bull, Ambrose Bull the uncle, Ambrose Bull the nephew, or someone else with another name - he testified for Abby Guy. As with the other witnesses, Waddell took him to the issue of Abby's whiteness, recalling an incident back in a court hearing back in 1849. "I have heard William Daniel say in court and to the Judge that no person except himself could prove that Abby had a drop of negro blood in her," said the witness, "and he could not do it without reference to his papers, and he did not know that he could do it then." This admission by Daniel was of critical importance to show that Abby was white, and showing that even Daniel himself doubted he could prove she wasn't.

Bull conceded that he did not know if Daniel was under oath when he made that statement. "He was talking to the Judge when I came in," the witness said. "He was talking in open court and apparently in respect to some matter before the court." The swearing of witnesses has always been a fundamental part of American courts, and it is likely he would have been under oath on that occasion. The jurors probably believed Daniel was in fact under oath at the time he made the statement.

This testimony of Keightly Sanders was supportive of statements already made by others, that Abby was white, and that William Daniel admitted it. It was a basis for Waddell to urge the jury later to disbelieve Daniel's own slave documents because Daniel didn't seem to believe them himself. It had the added bonus of apparently being under oath to a judge in an open court, so he was likely telling the truth at that moment.

Attorney James Yell did not regain much ground from this witness on cross-examination. Sanders admitted that on the occasion of that 1849 in-court statement that "I can not say what the question before the court was."[73] That was the end of his testimony.

Dr. Isaac Newton & Dr. Milton Comer

Waddell and Dubuose then put on two gentlemen who were medical doctors and considered to be expert witnesses. They testified about issues on which they claimed an expertise, namely, the racial characteristics of people. Dr. Isaac Newton, 73, owned quite a lot of land in almost all directions from Hamburg, and owned two or three slaves himself.

"I am a physician and have read physiology," he stated. "Physiology" was defined in the 1828 Webster's Dictionary as "the science of the properties and functions of animals and plants... what is common to all animals and plants, and what is peculiar to individuals and species." The word "animals" was broadly used in this context and was intended to include human beings. In other words, it was the study of people and how their appearance was alike or different from other people. In the courts of the South before 1861, people who professed these qualifications were permitted to testify as experts as to the physical characteristics of various races and whether a given person had African blood.

Just what the testimony by Dr. Newton was is something of a puzzle. What is stated in the existing trial record is extremely short and muddled and cannot be complete. "There are five races," Newton said. "I think there is but one race of negroes. The negro is the lowest in intellect." This opinion prevailed at the time and was the underlying rationale of most slave owners.

Dr. Newton went on to say that "color, hair, feet, torso and the form of the skull and bones furnish the means of distinguishing negro blood or descent." He said that "the hair never becomes straight until after the third descent from the negro, from either the father or mother's side. The flat nose also remains observable for several descents." That ended the summary of his testimony in the trial records.

There had to have been more to the testimony than that, such as a discussion of how he thought these things (color, hair, etc.) could distinguish between black and white racial features, so that the jury members could be informed as to what their observations meant when they had examined the appearance of Abby and the children earlier in the trial. Judge Sorrels had instructed the jury then to wait for expert testimony later, which was what was being given now. Also, Dr. Newton must have personally examined the features of Abby Guy and the children and testified about what he observed, discussing her skin color, hair, nose, and other features. Most importantly of all, he must have stated an opinion about what the race of Abby was, and that his opinion was that she was white. He had to have said something along these lines or Waddell and Dubose would never have called him as a witness.

Dr. Milton C. Comer testified next. He lived in Mill Creek Township in Ashley County. He owned upwards of thirty slaves, more than almost anyone else in the county and more than William Daniel. He simply stated that he was also a physician, that he had heard the testimony of Dr. Newton, and that he agreed with his statements. He verified and strengthened whatever credence the jury gave to Dr. Newton's testimony.

That, then, was the legal case presented for the freedom of Abby Guy. Waddell and Dubose had put before the jury members the best evidence they had to convince them to rule in her favor and to free her from slavery. There is always the attorney's fear that it is not enough, or that the jury did not really comprehend all of its meaning. But for better or worse, the presentation was over. Now it was the turn of James Yell to present the case for the enslavement of Abby Guy.

Chapter 4
The Case for Abby Guy's Enslavement

The trial was held four days before William Daniel's 60th birthday. He was been born in South Carolina in April 1795. When he and his family left Alabama and went to southeast Arkansas in 1844, he obtained about a thousand acres of land, making him one of the largest landowners in the area. They lived in the small community of Fountain Hill in the northern part of the county and owned land east and south of there. He and his much younger wife, Frances, had a somewhat typical nineteenth-century American family. By 1855 they had eleven children, some of whom did not reach adulthood. Their son John died in 1843 when he was almost two years old. They had a six-year-old son, James, who died a year later on June 20, 1844. Two months later, their three-month-old daughter, Martha, died. Those were hard times, and were common then. The family attended the Methodist Episcopal Church.[74]

Less than half of the white people in the South and in Arkansas owned slaves. Those that did usually had only a few. The typical situation was that slaves would work in the fields alongside the owners, or in the home with the women. Ashley County did not have large plantations where dozens or hundreds of slaves worked while owners had lives of idle pleasure. Within this context, Daniel owned more slaves than most people in Ashley County.

In 1850, when Sheriff Ducker came as the census taker to the Daniel home in Fountain Hill, William identified his slaves for the purpose of the census. Of his fifteen slaves, nine were male and six female. Twelve were listed as "black" and three as "mulatto." The oldest was a 55-year-old female and the youngest a one year old boy. As previously stated, none of these descriptions corresponded to Abby Guy or her children.

William Daniel did what many people did in that day and place - he owned slaves. Doing so had been part of Southern society generations. Within that context, he was perhaps not as harsh a character as others. An interesting fact was that on April 17, 1849, he was the first person the newly formed Ashley County charged with an offense in the court of the Justice of the Peace. "The county court issued its first citation, commanding

William Daniel to appear at the next term of the court... then and there to show cause, if any, why he should not be dealt with... for allowing his negroes to live without some free white person with them, to the annoyance of the neighborhood."[75] This complaint would not have been about Abby, who was then living with James Guy and raising her own family. Daniel's carefree conduct about his slaves was the opposite of the severe slave enforcement mentality that he was now showing in this case. It appears that a solution was worked out and the charge was dismissed.[76] The matter was not viewed by others as being particularly important, as the County Court (which was similar to a County Commission in other states) afterward appointed him to fill an unexpired term of one of its three members.

When William Daniel retained his legal services, attorney James Yell prepared a response to Abby Guy's Petition for Freedom, called an Answer. The Answer was simply a response to the statements made by Abby in her document. It said that Daniel had "all manner of objections to the many errors and misstatements" in the petition. It went to the heart of his position by saying that "Abby and her four children are not free but slaves and the property of William Daniel."

Yell's Answer for Daniel did make some interesting concessions to what Abby had said in her Petition. Some of the concessions were stated; some were indicated by silence. "It is not true that the mother of Abby was a poor orphan girl, living from place to place," it said, "but she was a slave and the property of William Daniel's father in her girlhood, and was raised by the father." His failure to say when "girlhood" began, whether she was bought at five or twelve years of age, makes the denial sound weak and vague on that point. The truth probably was that the Daniel family did not know about the mother's history prior to them buying her from slave traders, that she likely was an orphan girl when they obtained her, and that they did not know whether she was really of African descent.

The Answer explained that Abby was born as the child of a slave mother and that she was raised as a slave. When James Daniel, the father of William Daniel, died, "Abby was left as a portion of his estate" and was given by will to William's sister, Betsy Daniel Condray, and her husband, James. William Daniel purchased Abby from them on June 23, 1825, for $400, when she was thirteen years old. Sometime in the period of 1835-1837, William sold Abby to his brother, Nathaniel Daniel, "who never paid the purchase money." Many years later, on July 2, 1842, Nathaniel gave Abby back to William in exchange for the cancellation of the debt. It is not a surprise that the Answer did not address the statement in the Petition for Freedom that Nathaniel was the father of Abby's two oldest children. It was likely well known within the family that this was true.

Pounding the issue of Abby's slave status, Yell in the Answer said that "while she remained as the slave of his father, she was always treated as a slave and considered and known as a slave." Then William Daniel stated that he had "held and treated her for ten or twelve years as a slave before he traded her to Nathaniel Daniel as a slave." In the document Daniel used the term "the girl Abby" even though she was more than forty years old, using a demeaning terminology for people in a slave status, and attempting to convey to the reader of the Answer that she was in that status.

Abby Guy in her Petition for Freedom had said that she and her mother were given favorable treatment as slaves because they were white. The Answer did not address the whiteness issue but conceded the favorable treatment. "While she was with Nathaniel Daniel she might have been a favored slave, and probably was," it said, "but she was always known and considered a slave, even while living with him."

In her petition Abby had said that in his will Nathaniel Daniel had set her and her two children free. William denied it. He also denied that Nathaniel had ever made provision for Abby and the support of Abby as a free person, as she had claimed. He said that at the time of his death Nathaniel didn't even have the legal right to set them free because Abby and the children were by then once again owned by William.

Abby had asserted in her petition that she had been living free for several years. William Daniel, referred to in the Answer as "this Defendant," conceded that this was true. "This Defendant admits that the said girl Abby has been considered by him as of little value to him as a slave," he said, "and consequently he permitted her to go where she pleased for several years past." Even so, he continued, he "considered and held himself responsible for her, as his slave."

That benign neglect by William Daniel all changed when Abby "with her children ran away from the State of Arkansas, and not long since this Defendant found them in the State of Louisiana and brought them home." So here was a statement by William Daniel himself why his attitude toward Abby Guy had changed. He was angry because Abby had, in his view, taken advantage of the freedom he gave her by running away to another state, an act of defiance he could not tolerate.

He concluded by saying that "Abby was and has always been a slave, and all her children, and they are all now the slaves of this Defendant, and he prays the Court to return them to him as his slaves." The Answer was signed by the law firm of "Yell & Harrison." William Daniel signed a statement before the court clerk, Robert F. Holmes, saying that the facts stated in the document were true upon his own knowledge. The Answer was filed when the case was called for trial on April 4, 1855.[77]

John C. Waddell and Benoni S. Dubose made a motion to strike the Answer from the case, removing it from the file as if had never been made. Yell objected but Judge Sorrels granted the motion. The law did not contemplate an Answer in a freedom suit, and it, like Abby's Petition for Freedom, could not be read to the jury as evidence. The parties could not testify, either verbally as a witness on the stand or through their written words, in her Petition and his Answer. Both were under an equal disadvantage. The Answer was stricken, and Yell stated his opposition for the court record.

Despite its assertive rhetoric of slave ownership, William Daniel's Answer about Abby Guy was essentially truthful. His statements that Abby's mother was a slave when Abby was born, and that Abby grew up as a slave in the Daniel family, were true. Abby had said these very things in her Petition for Freedom.

Perhaps most interesting of all is not what Daniel said but what he did not say. He never denied that Abby was white, or that her children were white. He did not say that Abby's mother was not born free, something which the Daniel family could not have known about with certainty. All the Answer said was that Abby was "not free" because she was born a slave, had been treated as a slave, and was still a slave.

This failure to deny that Abby Guy and the children were white is of the greatest significance. Perhaps it was an oversight in preparing the Answer, which attorneys sometimes do. If so, it was monumental legal malpractice. James Yell, however, was an experienced attorney, and it is to be assumed that his failure to deny it was knowing and intentional. It is possible that Yell simply thought that it was not important to deny that they were white because he was going to have witnesses say Abby's mother was "mulatto," meaning that Abby was mulatto too, and because he felt that his case about being born to a slave mother was a strong enough point to win the legal case for his client.

Thomas S. Thompson

The legal strategy of attorney James Yell in this trial was to depersonalize Abby Guy and her children, to establish the mindset of the jury that slaves were not really people. "Slaves are property"[78] was the law of the day, and it was also the prevailing opinion among many, though not all, of the white people in southeast Arkansas. Once this position was accepted, then the next point would easily follow. Abby Guy's mother was a slave, so Abby was born a slave and had never since been freed, and thus was still a slave. The same was true of her children, who were born to a slave mother and had never been freed. The law concerning a mother and her children was that "if she was a slave when they were born, they are slaves."[79] End of story; nothing further need be considered; end of the lawsuit for freedom. That was Yell's case.

Yell started his case with the witness Thomas S. Thompson. Thompson was 42 years old, having been born in Georgia about 1812. He was a farmer and owned several slaves. Back in 1849, Thompson had served on the first grand jury of Ashley County. One of the other grand jurors with him then was Ambrose Bull, who now served as foreman of the jury. They knew each other well. Thompson was a Justice of the Peace and was active and well known in the community. He was of a stature similar to that of Abby's witness, Sheriff Ducker.

Thompson started by saying, "I know the parties, and have known Abby since about the year 1822 or 1823. I was, when I first knew her, a small boy and she was a little girl. She was then living with James Condray, and I first saw her at his house." Thompson was referring to James Condray, the husband of William Daniel's sister, Betsy, who had inherited Abby from her father, James Daniel.

"I knew her mother," continued Thompson, "or the woman who was reported to be her mother, and whom she recognized and called her mother. She was a slave and called Pally. We generally called her Aunt Pally." Thompson was being careful about his testimony. Of course, he did not know as a fact who Abby's mother actually was, so he made that clear in his wording. Yet his statements established the essential basis of Yell's case for Daniel, that Abby's mother was a slave when Abby was born.

Under the slave code it was a very strong point.

Throughout the South, slavery descended to the children from the mother and not the father. The rule was that if the mother was a slave when a child was born, that child was a slave, even if the father was pure white. This was because men wrote the law, because fathers were harder to identify than mothers, and because the fathers of many slaves were, in fact, white. This was something which those white fathers did not wish to acknowledge. It was desired by the slave owners that such children - their own children - be kept as slaves. Otherwise, there would have been an ever-growing population of free "mulattoes."

Perhaps the most famous example of this situation is Thomas Jefferson, author of the Declaration of Independence and third President of the United States. In the 1800s it was widely circulated but denied by his daughters that as a widower he had a long-standing sexual relationship with a slave named Sally Hemings. She was thirty years younger than Jefferson, and starting as a teenager she had several children with him. It is the conclusion of the Thomas Jefferson Foundation, after an extensive study about Jefferson, "that he most likely was the father of all six of Sally Hemings's children." This was supported by DNA testing, the Hemings family traditional oral history, Jefferson's documented presence at the time when Sally conceived her children, and the strong resemblance of several of the children to him.[80] Sally Hemings was a slave when her children were born, and so the children were slaves even though the father Thomas Jefferson was white and free. That was the way the slave system worked.

There was a much darker side to the slave mother/white father situation. Perhaps the Jefferson and Hemings relationship was genteel and genuinely warm, but that was not always the case in slavery. Other relationships ranged from the slave woman's choiceless submission to authority down to violence and rape. In a social system filled with ugly truths, this was perhaps the worst - the physical pillaging of defenseless women. At the peril of their lives and physical safety, both slave women and slave men could do nothing about it.

Slavery was destructive to white people as well as black. It fostered and encouraged an inward feeling of racial hatred in the masters and in whites in general, a personal quality that was contrary to their own best interest as individuals. It was enforced by a system of widespread violence and fear that cast an ugly shadow across the entire free population. And it led to a system of cruel sexual exploitation of black women that also degraded the white men who practiced it. The economic gains of slavery for white society were more than outweighed by the negative personal characteristics of hatred, violence and debauchery.

This sexual abuse of slave women by white men gave rise to a large group of people with mixed race ancestry. Under the law, "every person not a full negro, who shall be one fourth or more negro, shall be deemed a mulatto."[81] "Mulattoes" were as much slaves as full Africans.

What was left unexplained in the statute, however, was the status of slaves who were *less* than one-fourth black. They no longer met the legal definition of "mulatto," something of which Abby's attorney would have been acutely aware. It was an issue that Judge Sorrels would have to deal with when he instructed the jury about what the law was pertaining to Abby Guy.

It was within this race-conscious society and legal system that Thomas Thompson testified about Abby Guy and her mother, Pally. Attorney James Yell had the witness go into the subject of the mother's color. "She was a yellow woman," Thompson said of Abby's mother, Pally, "darker than white, a tolerably bright mulatto, and a shade darker than Abby. I cannot say whether she was of African or Indian extraction... She was called a mulatto and had the appearance of such."

Abby had claimed in her Petition for Freedom that she was white, and that her mother was also white but had been wrongfully enslaved as a young girl. That may have been true, and she had no African blood whatever. An alternative explanation of Abby's racial appearance was that she had an African ancestor several generations back, but by a succession of white fathers the African blood of the mothers had been diluted and was now visually lost. Starting at 100%, a family line could go in five generations to 1/2African, to 1/4, to 1/8, to 1/16, and to 1/32, and all physical characteristics by then being white. Perhaps Pally was at 1/8 with a "shade darker" appearance, Abby at 1/16 with no visible African characteristics, and her children at 1/32, all of which were far less than the "one-fourth or more negro" definition of a mulatto. No one knew then; no one knows now.

After establishing the claim that Pally had been a "mulatto" and therefore of black descent, Yell then moved the witness Thomas Thompson to Pally's status as slave. "When I first knew her," Thompson said, "she was the slave of William Daniel or his mother, who lived with him, and was under his control with other slaves of his mother, and was at his house."

Then he went on to Abby's status as a slave. "I knew Abby at Condray's," Thompson explained. "She afterward lived both with Nathaniel Daniel [William Daniel's brother] and William Daniel. She came to Arkansas from Alabama with William Daniel and I suppose he brought her. I never knew her to claim to be free. I knew her with Condray as a slave and knew her mother Pally as a slave."

This was the point where the jury was introduced through Thomas Thompson's testimony to Nathaniel Daniel, who had once owned Abby. The jurors did not see Abby's Petition or Daniel's Answer, so they did not know who he was until Thompson spoke his name. Abby had not been permitted to be a witness so she did not testify about him, nor did any of her witnesses. Perhaps, though, the jury members connected the dots between the name of Nathaniel Daniel and the names of Abby's oldest daughters, Elizabeth Daniel and Mary Daniel.

When Abby filed her Petition for Freedom, she was being very matter of fact when she said of her children Elizabeth and Mary, "the first named children above are said Nat Daniel's children."[82] Here is the Thomas Jefferson/ Sally Hemings situation, but with Nathaniel Daniel and Abby Guy. It would have surprised no one.

It is very likely, however, that this situation went back one generation further. James Daniel, the father of brothers William and Nathaniel, was the one who had bought Pally as a girl. Probably everyone in the courtroom that day intuitively knew and assumed, without testimony from any witness, that owner James Daniel and his slave woman Pally were the father and mother of Abby Guy. Because she was lighter in complexion than her mother, certainly Abby's father was white, and Pally's owner, James Daniel, is by far the most likely person to be that father.

That, in turn, made Abby Guy the half-sister of William Daniel, the man who now claimed to own her, and he was her half-brother. That explains why Pally was given favorable treatment as a slave, and why William let Abby live free after their arrival in Arkansas. They all knew the relationships. It made William Daniel the uncle of Elizabeth Frances, Mary, John and Malissa Ann.

This type of situation was not at all unusual. Thomas Jefferson's slave mistress Sally Hemings was actually the half-sister of his deceased wife, Martha. Martha's father, John Wayles, after the death of his wife, had six children with his slave Betty Hemings, one of whom was Sally. Such convoluted family relationships, where fathers had some children who were free and some who were slaves, and slaves had half-siblings who were free while free children had half-siblings who were slaves, were an inherent part of American slavery.

This half-sibling relationship between Abby Guy and William Daniel explains the bitter feelings between the two. Daniel, by his nature, had been lackadaisical with the governance of his slaves, leading to his 1849 citation for unsupervised slaves. When they moved to Arkansas in 1844, he simply let Abby go live her life. Daniel's statement in the Answer that "Abby has been considered by him as of little value to him as a slave and consequently he permitted her to go where she pleased for several years past" does not ring true. Abby and her children were as valuable as any other slaves of similar sex, age and health. What does ring true is that William Daniel had little stomach to enslave his half-sister. Abby was willful enough to push this freedom to the limit by moving away. Doubtless, Abby pondered why she should be enslaved when she appeared as white as, and maybe was actually as white as, her half-brother who owned her.

What Abby considered to be a free person moving to Louisiana was construed by William Daniel to be running away, as in a runaway slave. This made Daniel completely furious, likely feeling that his generous liberality toward her was intolerably abused by an ungrateful Abby. He tracked her down, kidnapped the family on December 1, 1854, and brought them back to Fountain Hill in chains. It was the half-brother owner, half-sister slave relationship that greatly embittered this legal battle.

The relationships go even further than this. Since William Daniel was the half-brother of Abby, then so was Nathaniel Daniel, the father of her two older children. That renders the Nathaniel/Abby relationship incestuous as they were half-brother and half-sister. Incest was another of the dark legacies of American slavery.[83]

With Thomas Thompson still on the stand, James Yell continued with his witness on the issue of whether Abby's mother was a white person. This involved issues about her appearance and physical characteristics such as her hair. "Pal had pretty straight hair," Thompson said, but then backtracked a little saying, "I think it had a sure curl. It was dark and it is my recollection that it was as dark as Abby's. I have seen the curl on the side of the head."

"She had other children besides Abby who were slaves," Thompson said about Pally. This is an interesting statement. Abby had brothers and sisters who were slaves but they had not asserted their freedom. Who the father of these siblings was is not known, but very likely he was the same as Abby's, James Daniel. Their racial status would have been the same as Abby's, but they did not have the audacious character that she had. Where these siblings were in 1855, whether in Alabama or Arkansas, or in or out of the ownership of the Daniels family, is unknown.

Thompson concluded his testimony by saying that Pally "always held herself a slave and acted as such. She and Abby always labored and conducted themselves as slaves in the family, with the exception they might have taken more care of themselves. She wore her hair long with a comb. She was a house servant and cook, and took good care of herself, and usually wore a cap. She always called herself a slave. She called William Daniel Master Billy."[84]

Through Thompson's testimony, James Yell had seriously challenged Waddell's case for Abby's freedom. Abby, the witness had shown, was light in color but simply, in the end, an ordinary slave.

Waddell or Dubose, on cross-examination, did what he could to salvage the situation. Yes, Thompson admitted, he was the brother in law of William Daniel. That family tie could impair Thompson's credibility and believability. Thompson was the brother of Daniel's wife, Frances. When William Daniel came to Arkansas in 1844, he was moving with his wife's extended family, including her parents and several married brothers. One of them was this witness, Thomas S. Thompson. Yell should have disarmed that fact by establishing it right at the beginning of his testimony. Most of the jurors probably knew this relationship anyway, but it would have been better to deal with it forthrightly.

Thompson also conceded that "I have never studied physiology or the difference in distinctions of races." Waddell asked him about Abby's color in comparison to other people. "I have seen many persons darker than Abby without any stain of negro blood," Thompson said. "I have seen women who were in the habit of working in the field much to get to be almost as dark as mulattoes, and as dark or darker than Abby's mother.... I have seen some persons darker than she [Pally] was that were said to be Portugese, and have seen others said to be Spaniards darker than she." He said Pally died two or three years before he left Alabama to come to

Arkansas.

"Abby came with William Daniel from Alabama," Thompson said, "and I never had any other idea than that he brought her, always looking upon her as a slave." When asked about Abby supporting herself by working on the farm after James Guy died, he said that "she went on the bayou to live, but I can't say when she left or whether she went to prosecute her own business or not."

The questioning in Waddell's cross-examination turned to Pally's hair color, and whether the hair was straight or curly. A lock of hair had been admitted into evidence and was said to be that of Abby's mother. Thompson wasn't sure. "Pally's hair had a sure curl. I think it was more like Abby's than that exhibited here. I can not say that the hair exhibited here is Pally's." The hair became a major point of discussion. "It is my impression and recollection that it was as dark as Abby's. I have seen the curl on the side of the head," he repeated. Thompson was clearly uncomfortable with this discussion. "I have often seen white persons whose hair was curly, as much or more than that of Abby's mother. Her hair was long, near the color of Abby's."[85]

Waddell finally got the definitive concession he wanted from Thomas Thompson. Speaking of Pally, Thompson said, "*I do not know whether she had any negro blood in her veins*. I only infer so from her being treated as a slave, and from her dark color... She was a very bright mulatto."[86] Notwithstanding this concession, Thomas Thompson overall had been a good witness for William Daniel. It was clear that he chose his words carefully about racial identification.

James Barnett

Attorney James Yell next called James Barnett to the stand. This time he put the family relationship out front. Barnett was William Daniel's nephew. "I know William Daniel and Abby, and Abby's children I have seen," Barnett said. "I have known Abby and William Daniel ever since I have known anybody. I am forty years old." Abby at the time of the trial was 44.

Yell took him through questioning to the central point of his case. "Abby belonged to James Daniel, my grandfather, when I first knew her. I have seen Abby in James Condray's possession as a slave, afterwards in possession of William Daniel," Barnett said. "I knew her mother. She lived with James Daniel, father of William Daniel.... She was a slave."

Then they turned to the issue of whether Abby's mother Pally was white. "She was not black nor white," said Barnett of Pally. "I can not be positive as to her color. She has been dead fifteen years." Barnett's discomfort was evident as he continued with his testimony about her racial characteristics. "She was not to say black nor as white as some," he repeated, this time with even more ambiguity. "She was not a dark mulatto." He said that "her hair was about straight," but then reversed and said "it might have been somewhat kinky. From appearance she was not white."

His testimony was not going well. "I can not draw a distinction between the negro and mulatto," he said, seemingly with exasperation, "nor between a mulatto and a white person. She was a shade darker than Abby."[87] Yell was probably glad to be done with Barnett.

Waddell then went on cross-examination. "I have seen many persons recognized as white as dark as Pal, the mother of Abby," Barnett conceded upon questioning. "There might have been a curl in the hair," he said, but then reversed himself again, saying, "I do not say that there was any kink or curl in her hair. I only mean I can not positively say there was not."[88] Waddell had succeeded in making Barnett look confused.

It would have been better for Yell not to have called James Barnett as a witness. He had floundered uncomfortably in this attempts to describe the skin color and hair of Abby and Pally. Barnett was dismissed from the stand.

James Cates

Yell next called James Cates to the stand. He was 59 years old. In the 1850 census he had been a widower with six children between the ages of eight and twenty-one. He appears not to have been a relative of William Daniel, but knew him back in Alabama when they all lived there.

"I know the parties, have known William Daniel and Abby for thirty years," Cates started. "I first knew Abby at James Condray's. I knew her mother who was called Pal. I never heard Abby call her mother." Like the others, he was being careful in his testimony, not wanting to overstate what he actually knew. "Pal was the color of a bright mulatto. I first saw her at William Daniel's. She was serving as a slave." The he turned to Abby, who, he said, called William Daniel "Master William."[89]

His testimony was short. It had value in that a non-relative verified some of what had been said by Thomas Thomspon and James Barnett. It didn't really add anything new to the case, however.

Kennon B. Thompson

The next witness was Kennon B. Thompson. He was another brother-in-law of William Daniel, and was the younger brother of Daniel's wife, Frances, and the earlier witness, Thomas S. Thompson. He was 28 years old.

"I know the parties," he began. Attorney James Yell took him to the same points to reinforce what had already been said. "I knew Abby in the State of Alabama," he testified. "I knew her mother, Pal. I knew her in the possession of William Daniel." When asked about Pally's color, he said, "She was a mulatto, a light mulatto, say of the complexion of a dark white person.... I think she called him Master Billy." Pally being the complexion of a dark white person was probably not what Yell was trying to elicit, and was likely a hurtful response for Daniel's position. One's own witnesses going off the intended script is a hazard that every attorney faces at trial. If Pal was the complexion of a dark white person, then maybe she *was* white.

Like his brother who had testified earlier, Kennon Thompson was obviously ill at ease with the racial testimony he was being called upon to give. All of the Daniel witnesses were noticeably uncomfortable when discussing race, color, hair and ancestry. The reason for this can only be speculated. Perhaps they did not like being involved in imposing slavery upon Abby, an apparent white woman whom they personally knew. They confidently told what they knew about her being a slave, but when asked about racial issues they faltered. *"I did not know, and do not mean to say, she had any negro blood,"* Kennon explained about Pally. "I only speak of her color as being dark, and as she was treated as a slave, I called her mulatto."

Again moving on to the hair issue, which seemed an important subject for Yell to prove, Kennon said of Pal that "she had long straight hair, and I can not remember of its being kinky or curly. It might have been one or the other so far as I remember."[90] His testimony ended and he was probably glad to get off the stand. Yell would have been glad, too. Yell had to have been feeling frustrated with the hesitant and ambiguous testimony he was getting from his witnesses.

James C. Burton

James Yell called one more family member, James C. Burton. He was the grandson of James Daniel and a nephew of William Daniel. Burton's deceased mother, Patsy Daniel Burton, was William Daniel's sister.

"I know all the parties," he said in introduction. "I have known Abby and William Daniel all my life. I knew Abby's mother. I recollect seeing her in my grandfather, James Daniel's, possession. She was always known and considered in the family as a slave. She called my grandmother 'Mistress' and my grandfather 'Old Master.' She was the cook."

Then Yell guided Burton's testimony to show that Abby had been a slave in Arkansas as well as in Alabama. "Abby called William Daniel 'Master Billy,'" he said. "When I first saw Abby in Arkansas she was at the William Daniels' home with his negroes, in 1844."[91] This firmly established that Abby had come to Arkansas as a slave.

With that, James Yell finished with his witnesses. Although the road was a little bumpy, he had done what he set out to do. He showed that Abby's mother was a slave and that she was darker than Abby. Abby was therefore born a slave, was a slave when she came to Arkansas, and was still a slave.

William Daniel's Documents

Attorney James Yell introduced into evidence the documents that supported his theory of the case that Abby was simply property, and that those who are born to slave mothers are themselves slaves. He introduced the will of James Daniel (the father of William Daniel), made in 1820, and admitted to probate, in Green County, Alabama, in 1821. In it, among various apportioning of his slaves among his children, James did "bequeath unto my beloved daughter Betsey Condray two negro girl slaves Rachel and Abby." James gave Abby's mother, Pally, and others to his son William for the purpose of supporting James's widow, Hannah Daniel.[92] In other words, at the age of ten Abby was separated from her mother as they were sent to different owners under the will. This was a common occurrence in slavery, and was surely traumatic for young Abby. Three years later they were reunited when William Daniel bought Abby, but were separated again when Abby was sold to Nathaniel Daniel. Finally, they were united once again several years later when Abby was transferred back to William.

William Daniel also introduced a Bill of Sale dated June 23, 1825. Slaves were an extremely valuable commodity and record keeping concerning them was carefully preserved. In this document James Condray stated that "for... the sum of four hundred dollars... I have bargained and sold to William Daniel one negro girl named Abby, thirteen years old, the right and title of which I do warrant and defend...."[93] It was just like a warranty deed for land, but instead was for ownership of a person. Now, thirty years later, Abby Guy was declaring that William Daniel had no title to her, to her body, or to her life.

William Daniel had in turn sold Abby to his brother Nathaniel, who never paid the purchase price. Nonpayment may well have been intended by the two brothers all along because the transaction was really the loan of a slave and not a sale. A Bill of Sale several years later was put into evidence, dated July 2, 1842, showing that Nathaniel Daniel conveyed ownership of Abby back to William. The document said that he "relinquished all my right, title, claim and interest in a certain negro woman named Abby, and her children Frances Elizabeth and Mary, unto William Daniel for the balance that I am due him for the purchase money for said negroes." Of course, the Bill of Sale did not say that Nathaniel was the father of Frances Elizabeth and Mary. He simply deeded his children away and that was the end of whatever relationship they had.

In her Petition for Freedom, Abby said that Nathaniel Daniel had set her and their two children free in his will and had provided means for her and their care. It is entirely possible, perhaps even probable, that Nathaniel actually told Abby, perhaps in pillow talk, that he would set her free, but then afterward did not keep his promise. In the trial William Daniel wanted to show that Nathaniel, in fact, did not set Abby and their children free by reading into evidence the will of Nathaniel Daniel, dated in August, 1842. The will did not mention Abby or her children, and would have clearly shown that Nathaniel, as an indisputable fact, did not free Abby or her two children. Judge Sorrels, however, excluded the will as irrelevant because it did not mention Abby or her children.[94] The will was also not important because by then Nathaniel did not even own Abby at the time of his death, and therefore could not have freed them.

At this point, attorney James Yell rested the presentation on behalf of William Daniel. Now the case was going to the jury.

Chapter 5
Whether Free Persons or Slaves

With the parties having presented their cases, there would have been a recess of court. The jurors would have been released for a break and to rest from their hours of intense listening to the witnesses. Meanwhile, Judge Sorrels and the attorneys would have worked on the jury instructions.

The trial had unfolded in an interesting way. Abby Guy presented one case that went essentially unchallenged by Daniel, and then William Daniel presented another case that went mostly unchallenged by Abby. Waddell and Dubose presented the case that Abby was white, and was accepted as such in white society, so she was in fact white and therefore free under the law. The jurors observed Abby's color for themselves. No witness said she wasn't accepted in white society. Yell presented the case that Abby was born a slave to a slave mother and had never been freed, so she was still a slave. No witness said she wasn't born a slave. Both positions under the law had a certain logic and truth, and both had supporting evidence in the trial. Both were essentially true. There was no reason to believe that any witnesses were lying; they were all doing their best to tell the truth, but they told different truths. Rather than being a head on collision about what the facts really were, they were the proverbial ships passing in the night. The jury members would have to choose one of those truths as their own.

Jury trials, then and now, in a very real sense have two judges. The trial judge is the judge of the law, and the jury is the judge of the facts. The trial judge is to decide what the law is that applies to the case, and to tell it to the jury in "instructions." After hearing from the witnesses and seeing all of the evidence, the jury is to decide what the facts really are. Then the jury members are to apply the law given by the judge to the facts as they find them to be. Their verdict is the legal "truth" that emerges from the trial.

During the break the attorneys struggled to get Judge Sorrels to accept their respective theories of what law applied to the case. They did this by proposing jury instructions that supported their positions. The Judge would then select the ones he felt were an accurate statement of the law, or make his own if he didn't like the ones from the lawyers.

James Yell wanted instructions that supported his argument and were based on the concept of slave status. His first one was that if the jury believed that Abby's mother was a slave, and that she was always known and held as a slave, then Abby and her children were then in fact still slaves. Second, if they found that if Abby's mother Pally "was a negro, or of negro extraction, and was always held and known as a slave," then Abby was still a slave. Third, if Abby was held as a slave for thirty years and acted as a slave during that time, it is evidence that she was a slave now. Fourth, in Arkansas a slave could only be freed by a deed of emancipation (which had not happened) or in a will at the death of the owner. Fifth, all evidence on physiology from the doctors plus the jury's direct observation of Abby and her children, was irrelevant and should be disregarded. Sixth, if Abby was legally a slave in Alabama then she was a slave in Arkansas.[95]

Waddell and Dubose argued for instructions about freedom and giving the benefit of the doubt to the plaintiffs. Judge Sorrels, for the most part, went their way. He adopted their proposed jury instructions and rejected all but one of the proposals by Yell. This was a significant accomplishment and victory for Abby Guy's attorneys, raising hopes for a favorable verdict.

Using the proposals of Waddell, Sorrels instructed the jury by reading the exact wording he wanted. He told the jurors that *"the only issue for the jury to determine in this case, and this they are to determine from all the evidence before them, is whether Plaintiffs are free persons or slaves."* In making that determination, they were to follow the rules of law that he was going to state to them. The phrasing of that instruction was very beneficial to Abby. The jury did not need to make a decision of whether she was white or her mother was white, but only whether she was free. No supporting reasoning or details needed to be decided; the general conclusion was sufficient for the verdict.

Judge Sorrels felt bound, as he should have, by the statutes passed by the legislature of Arkansas. This pushed him into two instructions about the "one-fourth negro" mulatto laws. He instructed that if they found that Abby Guy or her children "have less than one-fourth of negro blood in their veins, the jury should find them to be free persons upon that fact alone... unless the Defendant on his part has proven them to be slaves." There was undisputable evidence that Abby had been a slave before 1844, and that her two children born during that time were born into slavery, but notably absent was anything about her younger two children having ever been slaves. John and Malissa Ann's mother was not held as a slave when they were born. This could be the basis for a split verdict, keeping Abby, Elizabeth and Mary in slavery but freeing John and Malissa Ann. The evidence was that all the children had lived free for the ten years after 1844.

Then the Judge followed up with another instruction about the blood laws. If the jury did find that Abby or her children were less than one-fourth African, then the Defendant could only prove them to be slaves if their mother was one-fourth or more black. The witnesses had talked about Abby's mother, Pally, and her color. There was nothing in the testimony about Pally's parents' ancestry, or about Abby's father. There had been no proof in the trial that Abby herself was one fourth or more African.

Judge Sorrels then delivered a big blow against James Yell and William Daniel with this instruction: "The fact that the plaintiffs or their ancestors, have been actually held in slavery, or their words and acts in that position, are not conclusive evidence that they were rightfully held in slavery, and the only satisfactory proof of such right, is the fact that they are descended from a negress, or a woman one-fourth negro, who was a slave." The power of slavery did not make it legal simply because it had lasted for a long time. The long term enslavement of Pally and of Abby did not mean that they were lawfully held as slaves. It was a critical point.

The Judge did give one instruction requested by Yell. In Arkansas a slave could only be set free in a will or by emancipation by the owner. Impliedly, there was no such thing as setting a slave free by ignoring her while she lives her own life on the bayou.[96] This put into doubt the value of William Daniel's statements to Richard Stanley and Jeremiah Oats where he had said that he had nothing to do with her, and failed to claim ownership of her when specifically asked about it.

The next instruction, as requested by Waddell and Dubose, was for the benefit of the children. "Even though they should find Abby to be a slave, still the jury should find the other persons to be free, unless it has been proven that they are one-fourth negro, or are the children of Abby, a slave, or other slave, who is one-fourth negro." No one was arguing that Abby was one-fourth or more black. Her children would likely go free under this instruction, especially the younger two who were born while Abby had lived free. A verdict dividing the family with the mother found to be a slave while her children were free would be a difficult one for the jury members to make, but it was legally possible to do so. There is no doubt that if Abby herself was found to be a slave, she would nonetheless rejoice at a verdict setting her children free.

Lastly, Judge Sorrels instructed that *"every presumption, consistent with reason, should be indulged in favor of freedom."*[97] If any juror had any doubt of freedom or slavery, he was to come down on the side of freedom. This guidance was of the utmost importance. Abby and her attorneys had to have been pleased with this directive.

It is clear that the Judge had personally bought the case for the freedom of Abby Guy outlined by Waddell and Dubose. Why or how Sorrels arrived at this conclusion is not known, and it was probably never admitted or disclosed to anyone by him. His instructions were appropriately balanced between the two sides but he beyond doubt opened the way for the jury to free Abby and the children if it wanted to do so. Abby and her attorneys could not have expected anything better from a judge.

All the trial record states about closing arguments by the attorneys is that the jury retired "after hearing... the argument of counsel."[98] It is not difficult to divine what the lawyers said. John C. Waddell or Benoni S. Dubose presented the case for the woman and mother, Abby, and her four minor children. They wanted the jury to get past the legal technicalities and see them as real people. They were people who had lived free in this very community for ten years, which was the entire lives of the youngest two children. They were accepted by the jury's neighbors, who knew them and lived by them, as free and white. The jury members should accept them that way too. They had seen with their own eyes that Abby and each of her children had the appearance of white people, so they were white legally.

James Yell would have presented the well-known and harsh reality of the times. The petitioners were property, slave property, and that was all. They had been born slaves, had never been freed, and were still slaves. They were no different from any other slaves. The issues were as simple as that. Everyone had an interest in preserving the social system as it existed, and that included returning these slaves to their owner.

The attorneys were selling different visions of the same facts. Upon those facts, both sides were right. They all did their jobs and made their best cases. A reasonable juror on that day and in that case could decide a verdict either way with ample justification from the facts and the law. There is no doubt that in closing arguments the attorneys persuaded these jurors to the very best of their abilities.

In the end, though, it was up to the twelve men chaired by Ambrose Bull. It was "the right of the court to declare what the law is, and the duty of the jury... to... apply it to the facts they find to be proven."[99] What facts the jury found to be proven, though, were the jury's to decide. They did not have to explain their decision afterward, and actually could not explain in any formal way, nor could they write any reasons for their verdict. They would just declare "verdict for plaintiffs" or "verdict for defendant," and then go home. The jury could decide without accountability for the decision. Nothing would happen to the jurors no matter which way they decided. Waddell and Dubose were counting on them doing the good and gentle thing for this woman, Abby Guy, and her children. It was in their power to do it if they only would.

The trial record stated it simply. "After hearing the evidence adduced, the argument of counsel, and the instruction and charge of the court, the jury retired to consider their verdict." Judge Sorrels would then have gaveled the court into recess pending the return of the jury. At this point the parties would likely have been in an agony of anxiety. For Abby, nothing could be more important than her freedom and that of her children. With the instructions given by the judge, Dubose and Waddell would have encouraged her to be optimistic. Conversely, Yell was probably complaining to William Daniel and warning him that the judge had misunderstood the law and ruined the case. Surely, however, despite the judge, Yell and Daniel were looking to slaveholding jury members to protect and preserve the peculiar institution of slavery upon which the Southern economy was based.

The jury foreman was Ambrose Bull. The unexplained situation of there also being a witness named "A. Bull" has already been discussed. The foreman by that name was probably the Ambrose Bull who was about 48 years old and born in North Carolina. He and his wife, Sarah, had seven children, whom they were raising on a very large farm and acreage. They owned six slaves. On the initial creation of Ashley County in 1849, Bull's name was drawn as one of the members of the original grand jury. For the first county election in 1850, he served as one of three "managers of the general election," serving in that capacity along with William Daniel.[100] It is possible, though it seems less likely, that the foreman was the Ambrose Bull who was 25 years old and the nephew of the person just described.

In a very real way, every jury member had a stake in this case. As an institution of monumental importance and power in their society, slavery affected each one of them. For those who owned slaves, did they want their own slaves to win their freedom by court actions, or did they want to protect slavery and their ownership in it by shutting down every avenue of escape? Or maybe they saw it as just one case about one person's situation, which was unrelated to all other slaves. They may have seen what they considered as "the spectre of white slavery," which was to be avoided at all costs. Abby Guy, and even more so her children, may have been seen as simply too white for them to label as slaves.

More than that, the jury members had in their hands the fate of this woman and these four children who sat just a few feet away and whom they had closely observed. They had it in their power to free them or enslave them, a decision of the utmost consequence, and then they would thereafter have to individually live with what they had done. It was a sobering and momentous decision, one which surely hung very heavily on each juror. No one should think these people took their task lightly.

It is unknown what conversation took place in the jury room. Perhaps it was easily decided by these twelve men. Maybe it was a power struggle between factions of jury members, or a majority trying to convince one or two holdouts.

For whatever reason, or more likely for various reasons depending upon the individual juror, as a group they reached a unanimous conclusion. Once they did, word would have gone out to the sheriff watching over them, the clerk and the judge, and they in turn would have notified the attorneys and their parties to reassemble in the courtroom. Abby Guy, John C. Waddell, B.S. Dubose and their supporters gathered expectantly, as did William Daniel, James Yell, and their friends, and they all took their seats, nervously awaiting the announcement of the verdict.

The record states that the jury "returned with the following: We the Jury find for the Plaintiffs. Ambrose Bull, foreman, which said verdict was rendered in open court, and received and ordered to be recorded."[101] Abby Guy and her children were free. The slave owning white men of the jury saw them as people and not as property. As the judge had instructed, they had given Abby every presumption in favor of freedom. There must have been a gasp in the courtroom when the verdict was announced. Likely, there were cheers from Abby's supporters. After all, this case was about the most important of all issues, personal freedom. John Arnold would have been among those cheering for his lover and daughter.

Judge Theodoric Sorrels wasted no time in following up on the jury's verdict. He issued this dramatic order:

> "The right of each of the Plaintiffs, Abby Guy, Elizabeth F. Daniel, Mary Daniel, John Guy and Malissa Ann Arnold to freedom, having been well and sufficiently established by the evidence adduced in this case and the verdict of the jury, and the said Plaintiffs being entitled to Judgment of Liberation in their favor against William Daniel and all persons claiming under him... It is therefore considered by the Court that the said Plaintiffs, and each of them, be and they are hereby liberated from all service of William Daniel... and... are declared to be free persons."[102]

So here it was. Freedom for Abby Guy, and for the children.

Chapter 6
John Arnold

There was no way William Daniel was going to let Abby Guy walk away with her freedom without more of a fight. He was too angry with her to simply accept the verdict of the jury and the Order of Liberation of Judge Sorrels. His attorney James Yell made a motion to set aside the verdict for being contrary to the evidence, and moved for a new trial. Judge Sorrels said he would rule on the motion in two days.

On Friday, April 6, 1855, at the Ashley County Courthouse in Hamburg, Arkansas, the parties reassembled. Yell argued his motion for a new trial, saying that the jury disregarded the undisputed evidence that Abby was born of a slave mother and had never afterward been freed. Waddell opposed it. Judge Sorrels made short shrift of it. Denied. Daniel and Yell stated they would appeal it to the Arkansas Supreme Court and immediately posted their appeal bond. Abby Guy's heart must have sunk upon hearing this. The case was not over.[103] Daniel could have accepted the verdict and moved on with his life, but not accepting defeat in court was William Daniel's way. He had previously appealed a probate decision that had gone against him. Yell presented a document called a Bill of Particulars setting out his claims of errors made in the trial for the Supreme Court to consider.

There is nothing in the record showing that the Order of Liberation issued by Judge Sorrels was stayed or suspended during the appeal, yet the Judge followed the freedom statute and again ordered that the labor of Abby Guy and the children be hired out while the case continued. "It is ordered by the court that the sheriff... as he has been heretofore ordered, will continue to hire out the Plaintiffs to the highest bidder until the final termination of this suit.... and it is further ordered... that the Defendant William Daniel is not to bid at the hiring of the Plaintiffs or in any wise molesting them."[104]

It seems now that Judge Sorrels could and should have ruled that until such time, if ever, as the trial court verdict was overruled by the Supreme Court, the Order of Liberation stood in effect and that Abby and the children were free in every respect. Unfortunately, he felt compelled to continue to enforce the hiring out provision while the case was on appeal, even after a favorable verdict for the slave. As a result, during the time of the appeal, it was as if Abby had not even won the trial, and her legal status continued as a slave. She had been declared free, but this substance of the law was denied by the technical procedure of the hiring out statute. Such was the harsh enforcement of the slave code.

It was no surprise that John Arnold was once more the high bidder for Abby's labor, again frustrating the intent of the law to keep the plaintiffs enslaved during the pendency of the appeal. The case was then adjourned until such time as the Arkansas Supreme Court should make a ruling.

Abby Guy rose above it all, proving her amazing audacity. She immediately tested whether she actually had her freedom, and what the limit of that freedom was. Surely to the shock of many who were present and who heard about it afterward, Abby Guy and John Arnold stepped before Justice of the Peace James F. Ross. In the very courthouse where the trial was held two days earlier, and where a new trial had just been denied, they were about to be married. Right now.

Arkansas law was that "all marriages between white persons and negroes or mulattoes are declared to be illegal and void."[105] Was Abby now legally a white person? Technically, the jury did not find her to be white, but only entered a verdict that she was free. Judge Sorrels did not order that she was white, but only that she was liberated. Yet the underlying assumption of these actions was that Abby Guy was in fact white under the law. But what would happen to the marriage if the case was reversed on appeal and Abby was found to be a slave? This wedding was a bold, in-your-face move by the bride and groom. They were brazenly declaring that Abby was white and that this marriage was legal.

No one tried to stop it. Not Judge Sorrels, the slave owner who declared that Abby was free. He could have given the word and it would have been stopped. Not Sheriff Norris, who would have been present for court. Not William Daniel, who had been ordered not to molest her. He most likely just left the courthouse in a rush after his motion was denied. Not James Yell, who was likely muttering to himself in amazement. And not Justice of the Peace Ross, who was duty bound to perform only legal marriages, meaning marriages by and between white people. All he had to was say was, "no," he wouldn't do it, but instead he performed the marriage. The court clerk, Robert Holmes, entered it into the records. By these actions, Ross and Holmes were supporting Abby Guy and her cause of freedom.

So on April 6, 1855, with the power vested in him by law, Justice of the Peace Ross permitted Abby Guy, 44 years old, and John Arnold, 70, to make their vows and pledges to each other. The children would have been present, along with the attorneys John C. Waddell and Benoni Dubose. Surely others were there too for this happy event. Ross then pronounced them man and wife. The parents of young Malissa Ann Arnold were now legally married.

It was more than a wedding and a marriage. It was Abby Guy's announcement to the world that she was not a slave. She was a woman who was married as she chose, raising her children herself despite obstacles, and living her life as a free person.

Chapter 7
Treated as an Article of Merchandise

While John and Abby, who now took the name of Abigail Arnold, lived as husband and wife (though she was technically hired out to him as a slave), the freedom case for Abby and the children went forward on appeal. It had to be a dark cloud hanging over them every day, never too far from their thoughts. The trial was held in April 1855, and when the Arkansas Supreme Court met in Little Rock in July, attorney James Yell filed the appeal on behalf of William Daniel. Yell was a very experienced lawyer who handled both trials and appeals.

Not so with Abby's lawyers, John C. Waddell and Benoni Dubose. They were trial lawyers but had not handled appeals, and this was too important of an issue to be their first case on appeal. The nature of the legal work involved in trials is quite different from that in appeals. They require different skills, and not all lawyers are good at both.

Waddell and Dubose were able to get the premiere appeal lawyers in the state to represent Abby, the partnership of Pike & Cummins. On what compensation basis the firm came into the case is not known. Albert Pike had been a clerk in the Arkansas Supreme Court when he became an attorney. He was an officer in the Mexican War and was on his way to becoming a legendary figure in Arkansas history. He had a commanding presence, standing six feet tall and weighing 300 pounds, with a full beard and long hair past his shoulders. From their law office in Little Rock, he and Ebeneezer Cummins handled numerous appeals before the Supreme Court. On July 17th they entered their appearance on behalf of Abby Guy.

Appeals are now and were then excruciatingly slow in being resolved. The case of *Daniel v. Guy,* as it was designated because Daniel had appealed the trial court ruling, did not come up for decision for two years. In the interim between the trial in April 1855 and the Arkansas Supreme Court hearing in July 1857, much was happening the country. Political tensions were escalating, and the Southern states were becoming more extreme than ever before in defending slavery.

William Daniel's attorney, James Yell, ran for Governor in the August

1856 election. He was the candidate of the American Party, which was what was left of the collapsing Whigs. Yell received only 35% of the vote in heavily Democratic Arkansas, but even in defeat his fame in the state was growing greater.

The Arkansas Supreme Court met in session twice a year, in January and July, each time handling numerous pending matters. In January 1857 the Court heard another lawsuit with a slave petition for freedom which all the attorneys would have watched closely. Abby's appellate firm of Pike & Cummins represented the owner in that case and argued against the slave, something which Abby probably did not know and which would likely have distressed her.

In that particular case, "Bob, a negro, commenced an action... for freedom." The trial jury ruled in his favor and the owner appealed. The Supreme Court's general attitude and specific statements in the Bob decision were not reassuring for Abby. The three Justices were cramped in their outlook, concentrating on technical limitations rather than showing a broader vision. At Abby's trial Waddell had used statements made by William Daniel to witnesses Richard Stanley and Jeremiah Oats that Abby was free to do whatever she wanted to demonstrate to the jury that she was in fact free. In Bob's ruling, the Court discounted such evidence, saying that "we think the slave cannot establish his emancipation by the mere declarations of the master." Bob's case had involved issues about his buying his freedom, but the Justices said such an arrangement cannot be upheld because "both the money and the labor of the slave belong to the master, and could constitute no legal consideration for the contract." The Supreme Court did not defer in any way to the jury verdict in favor of the slave, which was reversed and sent back for a new trial.[106] This case was in no way encouraging.

Then, on March 6, 1857, the United States Supreme Court issued the Dred Scott decision, a Missouri freedom suit brought by a slave that had gone to the highest court in America. It was another disaster for Abby Guy's prospects. The case involved a slave named Dred Scott, who asserted that he was free because his owner had taken him into the free state of Illinois.

Chief Justice Roger B. Taney and a majority of the Supreme Court discussed in brutal terms the history of black people of America. "They had for more than a century before been regarded as beings of an inferior order," Taney wrote, "and altogether unfit to associate with the white race, either in social or political relations; and so far inferior, that they had no rights which the white man was bound to respect; and that the negro might justly and lawfully be reduced to slavery for his benefit. He was bought and sold, and treated as an ordinary article of merchandise and traffic, whenever a profit could be made by it."

Taney ended up ruling that since Dred Scott "was born a slave... then it appears affirmatively... that he is not a citizen" and cannot sue for his freedom in federal courts." The lower court ruling in his favor was therefore reversed.[107] The Arkansas Supreme Court had already reached his conclusion, ruling in 1846 that "free negroes, or free persons of color, are not citizens within the meaning of... [the] Constitution of the United States."[108]

The Dred Scott decision came at a time of change in the social and political climate of the United States. As the free states were becoming more populous and more politically powerful, taking control of the House of Representatives and threatening to do so in the Senate, the slave states were becoming more defensive and belligerent. Tension was rising. The 1856 presidential campaign for the first time saw the appearance of the new anti-slavery Republican Party. There was a nascent civil war already happening in "bleeding Kansas," fighting over whether that state would be free or slave. A South Carolina Congressman savagely beat and nearly killed a Massachusetts Senator over remarks made in a slavery debate.

Meanwhile, Abby's legal team was changing. After entering its appearance in the case in 1855, the firm of Pike & Cummins dissolved. Albert Pike left the firm and moved on to other things. Work was carried on by his partner, Ebeneezer Cummins, and a young new associate, Augustus H. Garland. Then, on March 11, 1857, four months before the Supreme Court argument for Abby Guy was scheduled, Cummins died. That left the fate of Abby and the children in the care of 25-year-old Garland. On July 3, 1857, Garland announced with advertisements in the newspaper *Arkansas State Gazette & Democrat* that "A.H. Garland... has in his hands the unsettled law business of Pike, Pike & Cummins, Cummins, and Cummins & Garland."[109]

Finally, in this political and legal atmosphere, the July 1857 term of the Arkansas Supreme Court began. Augustus Garland was already in town because his office was located there. When James Yell arrived in Little Rock to argue the case, along with other lawyers appearing before the court for that term, his and their presence in town was noted in the *Gazette* on July 18th.[110] Garland and Yell faced an Arkansas Supreme Court consisting of three men. The young Garland would be arguing before Chief Justice Elbert Hartwell English and Associate Justices Thomas B. Hanly and Christopher C. Scott.

Chief Justice English, 41 years old, was thoroughly knowledgeable in the law. He had written the 1848 publication called the *Digest of the Statutes of Arkansas* and had been on the Supreme Court for two years. After a few years as a silversmith, he started a law practice in Athens, Alabama, and served two terms in the Alabama legislature before moving to Arkansas in 1844 to start a career in Little Rock. His personal manner was described as genial and affable. He was a slave owner, and had written the decision in the *Bob* slave case issued in January that simply demolished Bob's suit for freedom.

Justice Hanly had joined the Chief Justice on the *Bob* decision. He was 43 years old, having been born, raised and educated in Kentucky. After college he moved to Helena, Arkansas, to start his legal career in 1834. He had served as circuit judge so he knew well what Judge Sorrels had been through at the trial. He served twice in the Arkansas Legislature before being appointed in 1856 to the Arkansas Supreme Court. He was known to have an aggressive personality and was a slave owner.

Justice Christopher Columbus Scott, 50, was the senior man on the bench, having served for nine years. Born in Virginia, he went to law school there and married the daughter of a judge on the Virginia Supreme Court. He then opened a law practice in Gainesville, Alabama. In 1842 a man threatened Scott's life and Scott killed him with a shotgun, so he and Daniel's attorney James Yell had something in common. Scott was acquitted by a jury but decided that his law practice in Alabama was finished, so he set up shop anew in Camden, Arkansas.[111]

Justice Scott did not participate in the case of Abby Guy and William Daniel. There are two possible reasons for this, both of which may have been true. The first was that Scott may have been a relative of William Daniel's wife. Scott's mother's maiden name was Thompson, the same name as William Daniel's wife and her two brothers who were witnesses in the trial. When Scott went to Gainesville, Alabama, he lived only eighteen miles from the area in which William Daniel and the extended

Thompson family lived. The second reason was that as an attorney in Alabama Scott may have represented the Thompson family or William Daniel, who lived not far away. Either of these reasons would have been good cause for Scott to step aside from participating in the case. Scott's non-participation in the case meant that to win the case James Yell would have to convince both of the remaining judges to support his position and overrule what had happened in the trial court.

It is unknown whether Abby Guy was present at the Arkansas Supreme Court at the time her case was heard in Little Rock. With her case for freedom being premised upon her being white and appearing white, it seems that Augustus Garland would have wanted her there physically in court for the justices to unofficially see and observe her.

The arguments were held, and the objections made by Yell at the trial court were heard again. As the one taking the case on appeal, Yell would have presented his case first. Abby's mother was a slave, so Abby was a slave, and so were her children. Yell complained that Judge Sorrels at the trial allowed improper evidence for Abby (the exhibition of their persons to the jury) and excluded proper evidence for William Daniel (his Answer and the will of Nathaniel Daniel). In addition, he argued that Sorrels had given bad instructions to the jury by using those urged by Abby's attorneys and by excluding those that Yell wanted. Finally, Yell asserted that the verdict of the jury was contrary to the evidence of slavery produced in the trial and the Judge should have therefore ordered a new trial, and the Supreme Court should do so now.

Perhaps John C. Waddell and B.S. Dubose were present at the hearing to observe. Augustus Garland argued in support of what Judge Sorrels had done at the trial. His emphasis would have been about people, about a mother and children, who were white and had lived free, and were now wrongfully enslaved. Garland argued that no mistakes were made at the trial in Hamburg. The rulings and instructions of the judge were proper, the verdict of the jury was sustained by ample evidence, and they should all now be sustained by the Supreme Court.

Justices English and Hanly probably asked some questions of both Yell and Garland. In doing so, their questions, manner, phraseology and temperament may have indicated which direction they were individually leaning. When Yell and Garland walked out of the courtroom, they might have had an inclination of whether they had won or lost. None of that is known now. The Supreme Court took the case under advisement and would issue a written opinion later.

That written opinion in *Daniel v. Guy* was issued in early September 1857.[112] Upon receiving it, Augustus Garland would have looked first at the back page of the opinion, down at the bottom. There he would have seen the very last sentence stating that "the judgment of the Court below is reversed... with instructions to grant William Daniel a new trial."[113] Abby Guy had lost. The jury verdict was thrown out. The Order of Liberation was canceled. It was recorded in the Circuit Court record that "the judgment of the Circuit Court in this case... is hereby... reversed, annulled and set aside...."[114]

Abby Guy and her children were slaves again.

Chapter 8
Racial Presumptions

Back on the Bayou Bartholomew, with sunken hearts Waddell and Dubose would have told Abby and the children what had happened at the Arkansas Supreme Court, and that they were slaves again. Abby must have been devastated beyond description. Telling clients this kind of news is also rough on attorneys. They, too, feel deeply for the personal impact of their work, especially when they do not succeed at such cost to other people.

At this meeting the attorneys would have explained the alternatives to Abby and the older children. They could either prepare for another trial, or they could remain slaves for the rest of their lives. Of course, put this way, they would go back to court. In any event, it was not in the character of Abby Guy to quit. She needed no encouragement. This fight would go on.

The good news was that the attorneys were willing to keep working for Abby's freedom and to try the case again. It is fairly clear in the record that John C. Waddell stayed in the case; whether Benoni Dubose did so is not apparent. At the beginning of the case in January 1855 Waddell had been a new attorney in the area. Now it was two and a half years later, and Waddell may have taken the case alone after this. Doubtless, he consulted with Dubose about it on occasion.

After the issuance of the opinion, Waddell, Dubose and Garland would have thoroughly reviewed the Arkansas Supreme Court decision. It's a necessary thing to do as a first step in building a new case for the second trial, but is a dispiriting exercise for lawyers to pick over the skeleton of a lost case to determine where they had made mistakes. Although a learning process, too, it is an unhappy one. Sometimes, though, it is redemptive. Once in a while, in a post-mortem analysis of the opinion, attorneys find it is the court that has made the mistakes, misunderstood the case, or ignored or changed the law. When that happens, it is a small consolation, but the second trial must still follow the Supreme Court decision whether it was good or bad.

Chief Justice English wrote the Supreme Court opinion, and Justice Hanly approved it. It set out in detail the testimony of the witnesses and the requested instructions given and not given by Judge Sorrels. Arkansas had been a state for only 19 years and its case law (the accumulated decisions of the state Supreme Court) was very limited compared to long-established states like Virginia and South Carolina. *Daniel v. Guy* presented an opportunity for the court, for better or worse, to address the subject and law of slavery in Arkansas.

Abby Guy's Petition for Freedom had claimed that she should be free because she was white and because even though born a slave, she had been emancipated in Nathaniel Daniel's will. No witness in the trial said that she had been emancipated, because Abby and the children as parties could not testify, and because no one else knew it or could prove it. William Daniel had shown that she in fact wasn't emancipated because Nathaniel had given ownership of Abby back to him prior to Nathaniel's death, and she had come to Arkansas as a slave. The Supreme Court went straight to the truth of that issue, ruling, "There was no competent evidence that she or her children had been legally emancipated."

The Justices were right. There was no emancipation proven at trial, and it had never happened. Abby Guy's road to freedom in a new trial now had to be based upon the sole issue of her and the children being white.

At the trial Judge Sorrels had instructed the jury that "the only issue for the jury to determine in this case... is whether Abby Guy and the children are free persons or slaves." The Supreme Court agreed that this was the proper statement of the issue. "The court correctly charged the jury," the Justices held, "that the only issue for them to determine was whether Abby and the children were free persons or slaves.... This issue properly turned upon the question of whether they belonged to the negro or the white race. If to the former, there could be but little doubt that they were slaves; if to the latter, of course, they were free."[115]

In deciding this issue, Judge Sorrels had further instructed the jury that "every presumption, consistent with reason, should be indulged in favor of freedom." The presumption in favor of freedom was upheld, but the Justices decided that this instruction as worded was in error because Sorrels "did not tell the jury what presumptions are consistent with reason." Upon this point the case was lost on appeal.

The Supreme Court used this occasion to announce the presumptions it found in the law, things that are to be assumed as true unless something significant shows it isn't true. In suits for freedom the Court said that there are the following general rules about people based on their race:

> "1. Where a person held as a slave sues for freedom, and it manifestly appears that he belongs to the negro race, whether of full or mixed blood, he is presumed to be a slave, that being the condition generally of such people in this State.
>
> "2. If it appears that he belongs to the white race, he is presumed to be free.
>
> "3. If it be doubtful, whether he belongs to the white or the negro race, there is no basis for a legal presumption, one way or the other, but it is safest to give him the benefit of the doubt, as the courts should be careful that a person of the white race be not deprived of his liberty."[116]

Waddell and Garland would have found some hope in these rules. All three points would be favorable to Abby Guy in a new trial. First, to be presumed a slave it must "manifestly appear" that she is black or of mixed blood. "Manifestly appears" conveys the necessity of the race being obvious, readily apparent, or plainly seen. Abby Guy was not manifestly black; the jury had found quite to the contrary, that she was manifestly white. Second, she appeared to be white, so she would be presumed to be free, which was what the jury had found. Third, if anyone had any doubt, they should give her the benefit of the doubt. The jury had done that. It had given the benefit of the doubt to Abby and set her free.

Vastly troubling, however, was the Supreme Court's lengthy discussion on the issue of a slave mother being one-quarter or more black, and about what the word "mulatto" meant. Arkansas law was that "every person, not a full negro, who shall be one-fourth or more negro, shall be deemed a mulatto."[117] Under this law, however, the status of a slave mother who is less than one-fourth black was unclear. The Arkansas Supreme Court here engaged in judicial activism and interpreted the law in such a manner as to effectively change it by the decision of the two Justices. They made these statutes subject to the general rule of slavery that "the child takes the condition of the mother, and if the mother belongs to the negro race, though but one-fourth negro, <u>or less</u>, and is a slave, the child will so be a slave." In other words, if the mother was a slave and had any African ancestry whatsoever, the child was a slave. The Justices held that "the legislature *meant* to embrace in the term "mulatto" persons belonging to the negro race who are of an intermixture of white and negro blood without regard to grades." In this manner they repealed the "one-fourth" wording of the statute and substituted a "one drop rule."

This was a devastating interpretation of the law, exceeding the wording of the statute and unsupported by any earlier case. The "one drop" rule was that any African ancestor anywhere in the family line, however remote, rendered a person black for purposes of slavery. Arkansas was the only slave state to adopt this one drop rule.[118]

To the relief of Waddell and Garland, the Supreme Court did not itself make the decision about whether Abby was white or black, free or slave. It left that determination for a new jury. In the next trial, it said, if the jury finds "that the mother of Abby and the grandmother of the other plaintiffs belonged to the negro race, and was a slave, this was sufficient to fix the status of the plaintiffs" as slaves. Also, the Court said that "if Abby was of the negro race, and a slave, her children were slaves." These words were brutal. If the next jury found that Abby had one African ancestor, and that her mother was a slave (as she was), then she would lose under the law announced in this decision. The attorneys had to explain this to Abby.

Yet there was still hope that the jury at the second trial would do what the first jury had done, find in favor of Abby Guy and her children no matter what the technicalities of the law may be. Jurors could simply render a new decision finding in their favor, without explanation of why or how they reached that conclusion.

On Yell's argument that the verdict was contrary to the evidence, the Court refused to comment on the testimony or its weight, saying that this was "a question for the jury." The Court had refused to throw out the jury decision and impose its own will. This was a basis for hope in a second trial.

The extremely narrow path to freedom was yet more narrow now, but Abby Guy was on that path and moving forward to another trial. John C. Waddell and Augustus H. Garland had an incredibly difficult task to make it work.

Chapter 9
David Roper

At the beginning of the lawsuit in February of 1855 John Arnold had hired the labor of Abby Guy and her children to save them from slavery. When Abby won the trial and received an Order of Liberation, he married her. Sometime between the wedding in April 1855 and July 1858 John Arnold died. He would have been about 72 or 73 years old. It was a tragedy all around for Abby. She lost her husband who had been such a critical support to her, and her daughter, Malissa Ann Arnold, lost her father.

John Arnold's death also had drastic ramifications because he had been the person who had hired Abby's labor when it was put out to the highest bidder. Since state law required in a freedom suit that the applicant's labor must be hired out pending resolution of the case,[119] Arnold had circumvented the whole intent by buying her labor and then marrying her. Abby had been free when the law intended that she be enslaved to the highest bidder. With Arnold's death this arrangement lapsed, and Abby had to be put back up on the auction block for her labor to be sold to the highest bidder. If her labor was bought by a stranger, she would in fact be a slave again. Abby Guy would avoid this at all costs; she was determined never to be a slave.

Once again Abby acted boldly to save herself and her children from slavery, and she had supporters in the community who were willing to help her. Just as the now deceased John Arnold had done before, David M. Roper stepped in to buy Abby's labor, and on July 30, 1858, to marry her. The bride's name, she told the clerk in Hamburg who wrote it down in the records, was "Abigail Arnold." Now she was officially Abigail Roper.

This marriage raises a host of intriguing questions. No labor bid document now exists, but the marriage record does. What makes sense of the situation is that Roper was the high bidder as well as the groom. Any other conclusion seems impossible. How could a free white man marry a woman who was hired out to someone else as a slave? The only logical answer is that he was also the one who hired her.

David M. Roper, 63 years old, was born in South Carolina about 1795, and had lived in Mississippi in 1850. His wife, Martha, had since died. Like Abby Guy and John Arnold, he could not read or write. He lived on eighty acres of land in De Bastrop Township, not far south of where James and Abby Guy had owned land. His adult sons, Thomas and James, had their own adjacent farms.

This marriage was even more daring and defiant than the one to Arnold. Abby had married John Arnold on the day Judge Sorrels issued an Order of Liberation from slavery, and no one dared to stop it. Now, with David Roper, the Order of Liberation granted earlier had been reversed by the Supreme Court, so her legal status was that of a slave. Yet she married a white man again even though State law still said that "all marriages of white persons with negroes or mulattoes are declared to be illegal and void."[120] Abby and those involved declared that she met the legal requirements, meaning, that she was white. Once again, no one had dared to stop the marriage. The truth probably was that, except for William Daniel, no one wanted to stop it. People were in fact supporting it.

Justice of the Peace Daniel Smith said in the marriage record that "I did on the 30th day of July 1858... duly solemnize the rights of matrimony between D M Roper and Abigail Arnold both of lawful age and citizens of [Ashley] County and did then and there declare them husband and wife *according to law*."[121] This young Justice of the Peace, 31 years old, lived in De Bastrop Township and would have known about Abby Guy and her court cases. It is evident that he supported her in her efforts. He declared her to be a "citizen," something the Arkansas Supreme Court and the Dred Scott decision would have questioned. He further said that Roper and Abby were married "according to law," meaning that he found her to be white as required by state marriage laws.

There can be no doubt that David M. Roper knew about Abby's history, that she had been born a slave and was in ongoing litigation for her freedom, and that William Daniel still claimed her as his slave. Roper either did not care, or she appealed to him all the more for these things. He, too, was brazen in marrying a woman in such circumstances. And so they thereafter lived as, and legally were, husband and wife.

While waiting for a second jury trial to be held, the Arkansas Supreme Court in the January 1858 term decided two other slave freedom cases that had implications for Abby as well. Attorney John C. Waddell, preparing for the another trial, would have been most attentive to what rulings were made in these new cases where the Justices applied the rulings that they had made in Abby's own case of *Daniel v. Guy*.

One case involved a 16-year-old boy named Thomas Gary. A Dr. Brown, engaging in the racial physiology testimony that was acceptable in those days, testified that he had examined Gary and "could discover no trace of the negro blood in his eyes, nose, mouth or jaws - his hair is smooth and of sandy complexion, perfectly straight and flat... his eyes blue, his jaws thin, his nose slim and long." Another witness, Dr. Dibbrell, said that "from personal appearances [he] would judge him to possess a small amount of negro blood, not more than a sixteenth, perhaps not so much; would not positively swear he had any at all." Thomas's mother was claimed to be white, but she had been a slave when Thomas was born, though she had since been emancipated.

The Supreme Court was ruthless with young Gary. Despite this description of his person as blue eyes with sandy hair, the Court applied the new one drop rule from *Daniel v. Guy*. Any African ancestor anywhere made him black for purposes of slavery. "Upon the issue, whether he belonged to the white, or the negro race," the Justices wrote, "we think the preponderance of testimony is, that he belongs to the latter. Finding this issue against him, the presumption of law, that he is a slave, at once attaches, notwithstanding the admixture of African blood may be but small." The Court cited the ruling in the Abby Guy case as justification for this one drop standard.

Then the Court hit the slave mother issue. "The evidence... connecting the complainant with the woman Susan, and that showing her condition of lawful slavery at the time of his birth, is sufficient to repel any presumption of freedom of the complainant." Again, they cited *Daniel v. Guy*.

This Gary case was devastating to the prospects of Abby Guy to be made free. Her case was no better than his. She was white in her appearance, but that didn't matter in the least to the Supreme Court when it considered Gary. She was undeniably the daughter of a woman who was a slave when she was born, just like Gary, which destroyed any presumption of freedom from Abby appearing to be white.[122] Waddell must have read it and despaired for his client.

Waddell, however, had done a better legal job for Abby than the attorney who had represented young Gary. That lawyer had filed his case as an equitable one, meaning that it was determined by a judge rather than a jury. There was no Supreme Court deference in that situation. Waddell had filed Abby's case as a legal (not equitable) one, invoking the right to a jury. He had the hope of persuading another jury to rule for Abby, something which the Supreme Court might respect on a second appeal. It was an important difference between the two cases.

The other Arkansas Supreme Court decision in January 1858 involved a black man named "Bob alias Robert Crow." Bob was of African descent and claimed to be free under a deed of emancipation from his owner, which document the trial court excluded from the jury. Understandably, with no document to show the jury members, they found in favor of the owner that Bob was still a slave. The court found that excluding the deed from evidence was a mistake and reversed the case, giving Bob a new trial.[123] This may have given hope to Waddell and Abby that the Supreme Court could sometimes be fair, even to a slave.

Generally, trial court judges whose decisions are overturned on appeal do not continue in the case. So it was with Judge Sorrels, who withdrew from further involvement. William Daniel had James Yell continue to represent him. Yell wanted not only a new judge but a new jury pool as well, so he asked for a change of venue to an adjacent county. The judge took the motion under advisement, and then on March 17, 1858, "ordered... that the venue in this case be changed to the County of Drew." This moved the case thirty miles north to Monticello, Arkansas, a town only about eighteen miles north of William Daniel's home.

There a jury would be selected from the men of that county, who were further removed from Abby Guy and from knowledge of the witnesses and facts. Drew County had about 5,000 white people and 1,500 slaves. "Monticello," said a newspaper article of the time, "is a beautiful little town, containing a population of about 400. It has a handsome new courthouse, three churches, an excellent male and female academy (separate), about six mercantile houses, and is altogether one of the most beautiful little towns in Arkansas."[124]

Josiah Gould, an experienced attorney who had previously served as an Arkansas judge and State Senator, was appointed to be the "special judge" to hear the case. Gould had been the Second Circuit Judge between 1849 and 1851 and was an appropriate choice for the job. The assignment for this single case was made by the Governor. "I, Elias N. Conway, Governor of the State of Arkansas... and reposing special trust and confidence in the ability and integrity of Josiah Gould, do hereby appoint and commission him Special Judge... to hear and determine the case.... He... is hereby authorized and required to perform all of the duties appertaining to said office of Special Judge as aforesaid according to the law and trust reposed in him." Gould took an oath of office to handle the case[125] and the trial was scheduled for late September 1858 in Monticello.

Judge Gould was 47 years old and owned about twenty slaves. Judge Sorrels had owned slaves but this did not stop him from being sympathetic to Abby Guy. Gould, however, had something alarming in his background. Twenty years earlier, on April 24, 1839, as an angry owner he had put a runaway slave advertisement in the Arkansas State Gazette: "$100 reward. Ran away from Little Rock, on Saturday night last, two negro boys, named Jim and Sam, aged about 17. Jim belongs to the subscriber, is about five feet high, slender, light black, and quite a pleasant countenance. He took with him a good pistol, and small brass powder flask.... I will give Fifty Dollars for the apprehension of Jim and Sam, if taken within the state... and lodged in any jail where I can get them. J. Gould."[126] According to William Daniel, Abby Guy had also been a runaway slave.

The distance from Hamburg to Monticello, although only about thirty miles, presented travel problems for the bringing in of witnesses for trial. On June 2, 1858, Yell made a motion to "take the written depositions of witnesses to be conditionally read at the hearing" of the case.[127] The word "conditionally" meant that the things said were subject to objection by the attorney on the other side if there was some reason to object, and the judge could rule on it later at the trial.

This sort of presentation of testimony is very much inferior to a live witness. The jury does not get the emotional impact of the witness, and listening to a document being read is something jurors don't always do, or do for long. Two months later, on August 14th, the same motion was dealt with again in court. Depositions could be taken by both sides if witnesses could not physically be present at trial.[128] The case was proceeding at a dreadfully slow pace. More than a year had passed since the decision of the Arkansas Supreme Court.

Ahead of the trial the court approved the opening and use of the depositions that had been taken.[129] Six days later, on September 30, 1858, Waddell made a motion "to suppress the depositions of Mary Washington, Samuel Mitchell, Jesse Daniel and S.S.C. Daniel." What new testimony these people had for the case is not known. The basis of the motion appears to be some technical defect with the commission of the notary certifying the depositions, but Judge Gould said that he was satisfied with the depositions and denied the motion. He allowed the clerk to amend the commissions and cure whatever wording problem existed. Waddell said he would make an "exception" to the decision, and thereby preserved that issue as the basis for an appeal if Abby lost the upcoming case.

Just as the trial was ready to begin, William Daniel's attorney James Yell made a motion to strike the trial date and continue it to the March 1859 term. Circuit courts met only twice a year, and this would impose a six-month delay on Abby Guy's freedom. Yell said that the delay was necessary "for the testimony of James D. Barnett, a material witness and who is not in attendance at this court." Barnett's testimony had not gone well in the first trial but Yell wanted him in court again. John C. Waddell opposed the continuance, but Judge Gould granted it. He did order that William Daniel pay Abby Guy and her attorney "all their costs at this term." Whatever money they had to spend in attending court and gathering witnesses was to be paid by Daniel. That was small consolation for waiting for six more months to decide Abby's freedom.

Looking to the conduct of the upcoming trial in March 1859, Judge Gould also ordered that the testimony taken in the earlier trial in April 1855 "may be read in evidence in any future trial." This testimony had been written in a document called a "bill of exceptions," which had been sent to the Supreme Court for its information on appeal. Gould said Yell would still have to introduce at trial and prove Daniel's "title papers" on Abby, which were the bill of sale for Abby from James Condray (Daniel's brother-in-law) to Daniel, as well as the document from Nathaniel Daniel returning ownership of Abby back to William. Both sides were given permission to take any other depositions they deemed necessary.[130]

With this continuance, Abby and the children lived in limbo for another half of a year.

While waiting for the trial, the issue of slavery in the United States continued to heat up politically. In February 1859 the Arkansas Legislature passed a law requiring all free blacks and "mulattoes" to leave the state by January 1, 1860, or be sold into slavery.[131] No other state went so far against African-descended people. The law applied to anyone who was one-quarter or more black. Hundreds of free blacks fled the state. Abby and her children claimed to be white but it had to have been uncomfortable for them to live in such a social atmosphere. In any event, they were not free to leave because they were slaves under the court order of their labor being hired out. Had they left the state, David Roper would have had to pay a penalty of $5,000, and if he did not do so, then the sureties who had pledged to back him would have been required to pay it. They would have lost their farms. Abby did not put her husband and friends in such a situation.

The second trial for the freedom of Abby Guy and her children was held in Monticello, Arkansas, on March 16, 1859. It had been four long years since the first trial in Hamburg. The attorneys, John C. Waddell and James Yell, appeared before Judge Gould and announced themselves ready for trial. As before, twelve men were selected from a jury pool of eighteen names.

A "jury of good and lawful men, to wit, J. S. Montgomery and eleven others who were duly elected, impaneled and sworn to well and truly try the issues joined herein and a true verdict give according to the evidence."[132] James Smiley Montgomery, the foreman, was a wealthy landowner who lived with his wife and four children east of Monticello. He owned 43 slaves, so he certainly had a significant investment in the slave system.

All the men drawn for the Drew County jury were farmers, half of whom were slaveholders. James S. Montgomery, age 31, Josiah White, 59, Green B. Jackson, 57, P. Alvis Thomasson, 43, Larkin Skinner, 62, T. J. Coleman, 62. and Benjamin A. Wyatt, 36, were farmers with families and slaves. Ezekiel B. Owens, 56, N.J. Thornton, 46, Shipman Denton, 54, Thomas K. Johnson, 34, Philip S. Wolf, 37, and Robert S. Bailey, 35, were farmers with families and no slaves. All were Southern born. Nothing is known about the other jurors, who were Isaac Lackey, George Erwin, Jesse Lord, [first name unknown] Reed, and William P. Bond. After the foreman Montgomery, it is not known which eleven of the other seventeen men were selected to serve on the Abby Guy jury.[133]

In this second trial the same essential facts were presented to the jury as in the first trial. Some witnesses testified in person. For witnesses not present at the second trial but who had testified at the first trial, the record of their testimony at the first trial were read to the jury. This included Sheriff William Ducker, who had died. Other new witnesses, who were not present, appeared by way of depositions read by the clerk. It was a very unsatisfactory way for the lawyers to present the case and for the jury to hear it.

It is to be expected that the attorneys presented the same legal theories as they did at the first trial. Waddell would have used the same strategy that had proven successful before, presenting the case that Abby Guy was a white person who was wrongly enslaved. She lived her life in ways that the jury would have perceived as how white people live, and she was accepted in white society as one of their own. The issue of her being freed in Nathaniel Daniel's will, which had been raised in the Petition for Freedom and found by the Supreme Court to have no validity, would not have been brought up.

Yell would have presented the testimony and documents that showed Abby Guy was born to a "mulatto" slave mother, so Abby had been a slave since birth, and so were her children. She and they had never been emancipated, and so were still slaves. They were just property, like all other slaves. Their light skin made no difference.

As before, both of the legal cases were essentially true. "After hearing the evidence adduced, the argument of counsel and the charge of the court, [the jury] retired to consider their verdict."[134] The jury had the task of choosing the theory it accepted and returning a verdict accordingly. It had the same difficult task that the first jury faced, deciding the freedom or slavery of real people whom they had come to know in the course of the trial.

This time, however, the jury could not reach a unanimous verdict for Abby Guy. They also could not agree in favor of William Daniel. The Court minutes recorded that, "Afterwards [the jury] returned into court here and say that they are not able to agree on their verdict."[135] The foreman, Montgomery, would have been the one informing Judge Gould of this predicament. Abby, the children and Waddell must have been mortified to hear that this time the jury could not reach a verdict. The trial had ended in a hung jury.

The jurors' private discussion is not known. How many jurors favored Abby and how many Daniel is not known. Presumably, some believed the most important fact was that Abby Guy was white, and others that she was born a slave and so was owned by William Daniel. It is not hard to imagine that jury foreman James Montgomery was likely on the side of William Daniel, but this is conjecture. Ultimately, after a thorough talking through of the issues, the differences among the jurors could not be bridged. Whether any juror voted against Abby on the basis that she was not white is not known. All the votes against her may simply have been on the basis that her mother was a slave.

Court was adjourned until nine o'clock the following morning. At that time the jury was discharged from further involvement in the case. The second trial had been a waste of time and emotion. The case was continued for a third trial at the next term of court in six months. It probably seemed to all the parties, attorneys and witnesses, that there was no end to this case. Such a feeling is common in lawsuits.

At that moment Judge Gould again implemented the labor for hire provision of the suit for freedom provision of the Arkansas statutes. He allowed for the older daughters to be hired out separately from Abby but required that the younger children stay with their mother. "The plaintiffs are ordered into the charge of the Sheriff of this County," Judge Gould directed, and the "sheriff is ordered and directed to hire out said plaintiffs to the best advantage for the time during the pendency of this suit." Then he directed that if Elizabeth or Mary were hired out separately that the employer must post separate bonds for them.[136] Drew County Sheriff D.S. Wells very likely would have simply continued whatever arrangement had already been put in place by Sheriff James Norris in Hamburg. David Roper had blunted this cruel hiring provision by hiring the labor of her and the children, and surely he continued to do so now. Nonetheless, the legal truth was that Abby and the children continued to be held in slavery during the pendency of this lawsuit.

After the hung jury and mistrial on March 16, 1859, there was no alternative but to hold a third trial. For Abby, she had to go on. If she didn't, she and her children would be handed over to William Daniel for a lifetime of slavery. John C. Waddell, practicing from the very small town of Hamburg, was willing to continue to help her. It is not known whether he ever received any pay for doing this work, but he was proving that his heart was in it. On May 21, 1859, he received permission of the court to take depositions of witnesses to be conditionally read to the jury at an upcoming third trial in September.[137] Two days later the defense received the same permission to take depositions.[138] James Yell was as determined for William Daniel as Waddell was for Abby.

Six months passed. On September 29, 1859, the trial records of Drew

County noted, "come the parties by their respective attorneys and... announce themselves ready for trial." Once again there was selected a "jury of good and lawful men, to wit, E. Henley and 11 others... to try the issue... after hearing the evidence adduced...."[139] Elijah Henley had been born in Tennessee in 1792 and so was 67 years old at the time of the trial. In Tennessee in 1850 he had been a school teacher, but afterward moved to Arkansas with his wife and grown children. Unlike the two previous jury foremen, he owned no slaves. His wife had passed away three years before the trial. He was not unlike John Arnold and David M. Roper; perhaps that was a promising sign to Waddell as he pondered the makeup of the jury.

James S. Grubbs was one of the men who came up on the jury list and was one of the twelve names drawn by the court clerk to actually serve on the jury. He was a 35-year-old farmer with seven children and a pregnant wife. For several years he had been a merchant in Ashley County near Hamburg when Abby was living with James Guy, and he likely knew her or at least something about her.

Grubbs was also one of the sureties who pledged his property in case of default by the person who bought Abby's labor after John Arnold died. That person, presumably her husband, David M. Roper, had promised that Abby would be available for trial. This very likely indicated a support by Grubbs for Abby Guy. James Yell knew of this situation, and when the jury was called in, he objected to a surety on the hire bond being one of the jurors. In modern times Grubbs would be dismissed in an instant from the jury pool, but ethical standards were not so well developed in those days. Judge Gould felt like this would not interfere with Grubb's ability to be fair, so he overruled the objection and Grubbs served as a juror. This same situation had come up in the first trial in Hamburg when John Arnold's surety William Morris was selected as one of the prospective jurors, but for some reason it was not considered a problem then.

The makeup of the jury was somewhat different from the one six months earlier. Three of the jury members were not farmers. Joseph Grubbs was a merchant, and William Payne, 37, was a "grocery keeper" who was married, had four children, and owned land but no slaves. James Rodgers, 27, was a farm laborer who was married with children but owned no land or slaves. The essence of the jury remained the same, however, with twelve free white men deciding the fate of one female slave.

Richard H. Cotham, age 29, Simpson H. Dabney, 48, Thomas Wells, 49, and William Allen, 31, were farmers with families, land and slaves. John W. Crook, 27, Joseph Shelton, 43, Jesse Whitaker, Sr., 55, and Chesley Garrison, 52, were farmers with no slaves. Isaac Andrew Jackson Handley, 44, was known nine years earlier to have lived with his younger brother and worked his land, and owned a few slaves himself. Of these men, Henley, Grubbs and ten others were selected as the jury.

After the swearing in of the jury, court was adjourned until the following morning. On Friday, September 30, 1859, the case went forward for a third trial. It appears that the presentation was again a combination of live witnesses, the record of testimony from the first trial read to the jury, and new depositions read to the jury.

In the course of the trial, physicians (probably Dr. Isaac Newton and Dr. Milton C. Comer again) "professed to be acquainted with physiology, and the distinguishing features of the races, stated that the color, hair, feet, nose and form of the skull and bones furnish means of distinguishing negro blood and descent." The discussion centered around "the peculiar formations of the negro foot" and that "an inspection of that member would ordinarily afford some indication of the race."

The situation was like the exhibition of Abby and the children at the first trial, but now it went even further. This time they "were brought into court for inspection, and were permitted to pull off their shoes and stockings, and exhibit their feet to the jury, against the objection of the defendant."[140] Yell this time conceded that the plaintiffs could be exhibited to the jury, but taking off their shoes and socks went too far. Judge Gould overruled him. Once again, this display of appearance before the jury members demonstrated the confidence of John C. Waddell and Abby in the "whiteness" of her features. The best evidence that Abby and the children were white was for the jury members to look at them and observe for themselves. Such was the law in that day.

Following the presentation of evidence, instructions were given and the attorneys made their arguments. For the third time they made their respective cases. Waddell would have again argued that Abby and the children were white and wrongfully enslaved. Yell would have again made the case that they were just property because they were born of slave mothers. Waddell and Abby, and Yell and William Daniel, were by now well familiar with these closing statements and likely very weary of it all, although inwardly still extremely anxious about the all important decision the jury would make. Judge Gould's jury instructions would have followed the Supreme Court guidelines stated in the ruling of the appeal.

For these jurors at this third trial, the importance and emotion of this trial and their decision was as great as it was for the jury in the first trial. This was their first trial, not the third. They, too, had in their hands the fate of this woman and these four children, real people who sat before them and who they closely observed. They, too, had it in their power to free them or enslave them. It would have been one of the most important decisions that any of them would ever make, and they would have fully felt the burden of their momentous task.

"After hearing the argument of counsel and the charge of the court [the jury] retired to consider their verdict," the record says. For clients and attorneys, time hangs heavy - very heavy - when a jury is deliberating. It's hard to think of anything else except what could possibly be going on in the jury room. Then word came that they had reached a verdict, and the judge, attorneys and parties scrambled back to their places in the courtroom to hear the word. This third jury "returned in to court the following verdict, to wit; 'We the Jury find for the plaintiffs. E. Henley, foreman.'"

Abby Guy had won again. The thrill and elation of winning at this third trial must have been as great as winning the first one, but this time with an even larger sense of relief. Judge Gould then issued an Order of Liberation declaring that "Abby Guy, Elizabeth F. Daniel, Mary Daniel, John Guy and Malissa Ann Arnold go hence [and] are liberated from all claims of... William Daniel."[141] He ordered that Daniel pay all of Abby's costs expended in the suit.

After the verdict went against him again, Yell predictably moved for a new trial. He argued to Judge Gould what he had previously urged to Judge Sorrels, "that there was a total want of evidence to support the verdict."[142] Judge Gould may or may not have agreed with Yell, but he was not going to disturb the jury verdict. The finding of facts, of whether Abby and the children were white, was the duty of the jury and not of the judge.

There was another basis for the motion for a new trial. In the course of the proceedings, or shortly afterward, Yell learned that the juror James S. Grubbs had before the trial expressed an opinion that "that he did not think that Daniel could ever get a verdict against Abby Guy."[143] Grubbs, Yell said, should never have been on the jury.

The hapless Grubbs was caught in a courtroom furor in which he did not know what to do. He gave an affidavit to Yell "stating that he had formed and expressed an opinion in the case from rumor... but that he had no idea at the time that he would ever be sworn as a juror in the case." Then he gave another affidavit to Waddell in which he said that it "was not such an opinion as would have prevented him from finding a verdict according to the evidence." Both affidavits were probably true.

On this issue Waddell had on his side a recent decision of the Arkansas Supreme Court. "Where a juror admits that he has formed an opinion as to... guilt... he is incompetent" to serve as a juror, the Court said, *unless* "it appears that the opinion was founded on rumor, and was not such as to bias or prejudice his mind."[144] In his second affidavit Grubbs said his opinion was based on rumor but he could still be fair, so he met the requirement to continue to serve on the jury.

Judge Gould was again not concerned about Mr. Grubbs because after the trial it was too late for Yell to bring up such an objection. The Arkansas Supreme Court had held in another case that a party "will not, after conviction, be allowed to make the objection that the juror had formed and expressed an opinion adverse to him, as a ground for a new trial."[145] It was too late to make this claim, and Yell should have learned about it and brought his objection up earlier.[146] The motion for a new trial was denied. Grubbs probably went home hoping that he would never be called for jury duty again.

James Yell was immediately on his feet, stating that this case would be appealed to the Arkansas Supreme Court. Abby surely felt heartsick to hear that. It had happened before, but would this case never end?

Then came the revenge of William Daniel. Even though Abby Guy and the children had been declared free by a second jury and ordered liberated for a second time, Judge Gould said that they "are ordered into the charge of the Sheriff... who is directed to hire out said Plaintiffs to the best advantage."[147] Through this hiring out of labor, the slavery of Abby Guy was continued, though husband David Roper was still there to do the hiring.

Chapter 10
A Warmth of Expression

While the third jury trial was waiting for its scheduled date in late September of 1859, William Daniel and his large family moved into a new home east of Fountain Hill. He was prospering and doing well. The truth was that he did not need Abby Guy and her children as his slaves. He had not used her as a slave for fifteen years, and had many other slaves on hand. His life was going very well. For him, this extended legal battle with Abby was simply a point of pride, or simply meanness, a grudge match that he was determined to win. But for Abby this was a ruthless threat to her freedom and that of her children. Their entire lives were at stake. The battle was a sideshow for Daniel; it was everything for Abby.

As before, the wait to be heard before the Arkansas Supreme Court was agonizingly slow. During this time of waiting it is no exaggeration to say that the United States as a country was falling to pieces over slavery, the very issue that Abby was caught up in. Though completely out of her control, her timing could not have been worse. Her case was coming up at the very moment that the South was going into a belligerent siege mentality to protect slavery.

A month after the third trial, in October 1859, abolitionist John Brown made a raid on Harper's Ferry, Virginia, to incite a slave revolt. The uprising he hoped for didn't happen, and Brown was hanged on December 2nd. There was an uproar all over the nation as divisions over slavery grew to new levels of anger. Civil war was coming into view.

The collapse of the American political system unfolded during the presidential election of 1860, which was another year of waiting for Abby Guy's appeal. The Democratic Party split over slavery into Northern and Southern factions with each running its own presidential candidates, Senator Stephen A. Douglas and Vice President John C. Breckinridge, respectively. The anti-slavery Republican Party ran Abraham Lincoln for President, but he was not even on the ballot in Arkansas and other Southern states. A remnant of the old Whigs, the Constitutional Union Party, ran John Bell as a compromise and peace candidate.

William Daniel's attorney, James Yell, was a presidential elector for Bell in Arkansas and campaigned actively for him. Yell's name was often in the paper as a Bell supporter, and he spoke for him throughout the state, including at a rally in Hamburg. Surely Abby and David Roper did not attend. Yell's efforts were in vain. Breckinridge carried Arkansas with 53% of the vote to 37% for Bell and 10% for Douglas. Lincoln had no support or votes in Arkansas, but nationally he won a majority of the votes in the Electoral College and so was elected President of the United States. Judge Sorrels was one of the Arkansas presidential electors for Breckinridge.

Criticizing Lincoln as a "black Republican," and viewing the new President-elect as an intolerable burden, South Carolina seceded from the Union on December 20, 1860. Yell, the senior general in the Arkansas militia, now zealously called for Arkansas to also secede. Inflamed though he was with the national political situation, Yell focused his attention and attended the Arkansas Supreme Court session to argue against the slave woman Abby Guy being freed.

In the midst of secession and talk of war, the second Abby Guy appeal, along with numerous other pending lawsuits, was heard by the Arkansas Supreme Court in January 1861. The session began on Monday, January 7th, and on Wednesday Mississippi seceded from the Union. On Thursday Florida seceded, and Alabama on Friday. Other Southern states were debating what course to take. Passionate political controversy was sweeping over the people of Arkansas.

"The January term of the Supreme Court... is now in session," noted the *Arkansas State Gazette* on page 2 of the newspaper. The front page that day was filled with news of "Southern Independence" and "The State of the Union." There was talk of which way Arkansas should go on secession and whether there would be war. "The shadows and gloom which rest upon this once proud and happy government are by no means rapidly disappearing," reported the *Gazette*.[148] So, in the midst of looming disunion and possible civil war, the lawyers and judges had to turn from the excitement in the news and deal with the everyday lawsuits that were now scheduled for hearing. People still had disagreements to be resolved, and lawyers still had to make a living.

In the hearing at the Supreme Court on this second appeal, James Yell once again argued the case for William Daniel. Augustus Garland appeared again for Abby Guy. It seems likely that John C. Waddell, who had by then been admitted to appellate practice, was in attendance, too.

The judges on the appeal this time were somewhat different. Chief Justice Elbert H. English, who had written the first opinion, was still on the bench. Justice Thomas Hanley, who had joined English in the reversal of Abby Guy's favorable jury verdict was now gone, replaced by Freeman W. Compton. Justice Christopher Columbus Scott, who had not participated in the first case for conflict of interests reasons, was gone, too. He was succeeded by Hulbert F. Fairchild.

Justice Compton was 36 years old and practiced law in a rural area of Dallas County, Arkansas. He owned twenty slaves. Although he was reported in the papers to be present for the court session, for reasons not known Compton did not participate in the Abby Guy case.

Justice Fairchild had a different background from everyone else involved in the legal proceedings in the case of Abby Guy. He was a Northerner, born and raised in New York. He was educated in Massachusetts, where his wife was born. In 1838 the young couple went to Louisville so he could study law. Upon his admission to the bar in 1841, they moved to Pocahontas, Arkansas, and then four years later to Batesville. They adopted the Southern lifestyle and owned seven slaves.

In the 1850 census Fairchild and his wife had three children, Adaline, 12, Fannie, 7, and William, 2. Over the course of the next ten years, all three children died. Another daughter born after 1850 also died. The couple was childless as court convened for the January 1861 term of the Arkansas Supreme Court. How or if this would impact his view of the case can only be speculated upon.

As the attorney on appeal wanting to overturn the decision in the trial court, James Yell would have spoken first. Chief Justice English and Justice Fairchild were very much aware of the issue at stake. "It is manifest, from the testimony introduced upon the trial" they wrote afterward, "that the leading point of controversy in the case was whether the plaintiffs belonged to the white or negro race." Their framing of the issue in that manner showed their take on the case. They did not say that the leading point was whether Abby's mother was a slave when Abby was born, which was the method of analysis Yell wanted them to apply.

Yell argued "with much warmth of expression," the Court noted, "that the court committed a gross error in permitting Abby and the children to take off their shoes and stockings, and exhibit their bare feet for the observation of the jury." He also complained about the instructions given by Judge Gould, and about James S. Grubbs serving on the jury when he had been a surety on the bond for her appearance and had expressed a pre-trial opinion that Abby would win the case. Lastly, Yell argued that the jury verdict was unsupported by the evidence.

It is not known whether Abby Guy was present at the hearing. Again, it seems that it would have been wise to let the justices see her racial appearance for themselves. Augustus Garland argued that no errors were made by the trial court, and that there was ample evidence to support the jury decision, so the Court should affirm the judgment of the trial court judge and jury. If the Justices did that, Abby Guy and her children would be permanently free, beyond all reach of slavery. It is certain that Garland wanted to avoid another reversal on appeal and a fourth jury trial.

No decision was made on the day of the hearing. The Arkansas Supreme Court simply took the case under advisement and went on to the next item on the calendar. The Justices would discuss the case among themselves and issue a written decision later.

When at last the decision was issued, probably in late February of 1861, Augustus Garland would have done what he did on the case four years earlier. He would first have looked at the last page of the opinion, then down at the last line. There was the decision: "The judgment must be affirmed." Instantly he knew that the jury verdict and trial court were upheld. Abby Guy was finally, legally free. Elizabeth Daniel, Mary Daniel, John Guy and Malissa Ann Arnold were free. There was no appeal from this final decision of liberation.

By far the most important factor in reaching this outcome was the Court's decision to defer to, respect and uphold the jury verdict. The jury, the Justices said, acted "through reluctance to sanction the enslaving of persons, who, to all appearance, were of the white race, and, for many years before suit, had acted as free persons and been treated as such." The jury had ignored all of Yell's proof about a "mulatto" slave mother, and about Abby being born in slavery and never emancipated.

It is "the province of the jury to pass upon the weight of the evidence," the Justices ruled. They personally would have supported Yell's position enforcing slavery, but they were not the jury. "It is possible that the jury found against the preponderance of the evidence," they said, but "we can not... award a new trial because of an impression on our part that the verdict may have been contrary to the weight of the evidence." It is remarkable that the Court, in its own view of the facts, allowed the jury to disregard the one drop of African blood rule of slavery it had pronounced in Abby's first case.

It is also amazing that the Arkansas Supreme Court took this enlightened approach and gave Abby Guy her freedom at the exact moment when, over the issue of slavery, the United States was dissolving into two countries and war. The arguments had taken place during the very week when Southern states were seceding, when the attention of everyone, especially lawyers and judges, was diverted to exciting national and state news. Chief Justice English and Justice Fairchild had kept their focus on the matter at hand, Abby Guy's Petition for Freedom.

Augustus Garland, who lived in Little Rock, would have gotten the news first and sent it immediately on to John C. Waddell in Hamburg. When Waddell told Abby the news, the thrilling joy and relief that she felt must have been profound. Abby and the children would not be going back in chains to William Daniel. Abby could now put down the great burden of tension she had carried for six long, excruciating years.

James Yell would have sent word to William Daniel in Fountain Hill that he had lost and that Abby Guy and the children were free. Daniel may have considered it a bitter pill to swallow, or perhaps he just shrugged his shoulders. He didn't like losing, especially to Abby, but after all, this series of trials and appeals was not central to his life. He had plenty of other slaves. The whole six-year litigation had only been a point of pride and a low-stakes game for him. He would go ahead with his life as if this lawsuit had never happened.

Garland's and Waddell's review of the Supreme Court written opinion would have been a far happier exercise than it had been four years earlier. In its decision, which was much shorter than the first, the Court simply referenced the first case for a statement of the facts, witness testimony and evidence. On Yell's first complaint about the jury seeing the feet of the plaintiffs, the Court had no concern. "In a suit for freedom, where the leading matter in controversy was, whether the plaintiffs belonged to the white or negro race, and they were introduced for the inspection of the jury, it was not improper for the court to permit them to pull off their shoes and stockings and exhibit their bare feet to the jury, in order that they might observe their formation, it being proven by competent witnesses, and attested by experience, that the formation of the negro foot is peculiar."[149] They found no error in Judge Gould's ruling on this point.

Despite Yell's arguments, the Justices found that the jury instructions were "substantially in accordance with the principles of law settled by this court when the case was here before." Yell also failed to convince the Court that James S. Grubbs should not have been on the jury. "Where the plaintiffs in a suit for freedom, are hired out by the sheriff, pending the suit, a surety in the bond of the hirer... is not incompetent to serve as a juror on the trial." It was a minor issue to them.

There is a remarkable truth that needs to be observed about this unlikely result of a slave woman winning freedom in court. Except for James Yell, who was hired to represent the interests of William Daniel and was ethically bound to do so, every lawyer, trial judge and Supreme Court Justice in the case, the witnesses that Abby called, all twenty-four jurors from the two trials that she won, and an unknown number on the hung jury, acted against the overwhelming slave interests of the society in which they lived. Many of them acted against their own individual personal interest as slave owners. Each and all of them were personally fair minded, and honored what Judge Sorrels expressed in a jury instruction at the first trial six years earlier, that every presumption should be indulged in favor of freedom. The legal team of John C. Waddell, Benoni S. Dubose and Augustus H. Garland had found a way to put it all together.

So ended Abby Guy's Petition for Freedom. Hard fought though it was, it was a success beyond measure. Improbable as her prospects had been, this woman in a 19th century man's world, this slave in a society ruthlessly run by masters, this illiterate person in a legal system ruled by law books, had taken on the mighty and powerful slave establishment and had defeated it, winning freedom for herself and her children.

Chapter 11
Two Mares and a Colt

When word reached her in February of 1861 that she was free, Abigail Roper (as she then called herself) was not done with William Daniel. He had wronged her by enslaving her and her children in December 1854, and he had also wronged her by taking from her the personal property she had owned at that time. It is understandable that she was everlastingly angry at him. He had put her and her children through years of legal and emotional torment. Now, to express her justified wrath, she was fiercely determined to right one last injustice inflicted by Daniel.

America at that time was cascading headlong into civil war. Several weeks after the Supreme Court decision in favor of Abby, Confederate batteries opened fire on Fort Sumter, causing President Abraham Lincoln to call for 75,000 volunteers to put down the rebellion. This prompted Arkansas to secede from the Union on May 6th and join the Confederacy. Abby, without moving, now lived in another country, the Confederate States of America. On July 21st the Battle of Bull Run in Virginia was the first major clash of arms. The Southern troops were victorious, and spirits were running high throughout the new nation.

All of this didn't much phase Abby. She simply wanted justice from William Daniel, but was prevented from suing him for money damages for having enslaved her and having disrupted her life and the lives of her children. "In actions prosecuted under this act," Arkansas law stated, "the plaintiff shall not recover any damages."[150] That wording was plain enough; the injustice of it was overwhelming. Behind that law, William Daniel had enslaved five free-living people, causing extreme distress and hardship for six years, and for which he was immune from all liability. Of course, it must be remembered that the slave system and its laws were not instituted to achieve justice for slaves, even where it was ultimately found that the enslavement was wrong. The laws protected slave owners.

But one thing Abby could do was sue William Daniel for the property he took from her back in December of 1854. At that time she consulted with attorneys on what to do, including the ever faithful attorney and friend,

John C. Waddell. Slaves could not sue white people for any reason except for freedom. Waddell had advised her to wait until she was declared free by a court and then afterward file a lawsuit for her property. She followed this advice and waited for six years, and now she was free, including free to sue. She headed for court again. On August 1, 1861, she filed a second lawsuit against William Daniel. John C. Waddell once again appeared as her attorney. Now that the time had come when she could sue, he probably felt he had to stay in the case with her. More than that, after all these years he was very dedicated to obtaining justice for Abby.

The complaint charged "that when the defendant reduced her and her children to slavery, William Daniel took from her two mares and a colt, a yoke of oxen and a cart, which were property of her own acquisition, and to which William Daniel had no title."[151] Now she wanted them back. Daniel, upon losing the case for Abby's enslavement, could have simply returned them, accepting what had happened and saving the trouble of another lawsuit. But that was not his way. His way was personal strife and fighting it out to the last legal step. Waddell likely demanded the return of these animals and equipment and Daniel either refused or ignored him, so Abby filed a second lawsuit in the Circuit Court in Hamburg.

James Yell did not become involved in this new case, but his former partner Robert Hutchinson appeared for William Daniel. He was then in the firm of Johnston & Hutchinson, which may have had an office in Hamburg. He made a motion to dismiss the complaint on the basis of a three year statute of limitation for such a claim, saying that too much time had passed since the event had happened and that Abby's claim was therefore barred. Waddell asked for an injunction to prohibit Daniel from raising that defense because Abby as a slave could not bring the suit until she was declared free, which had occurred only a few months earlier. Her lawsuit was valid, he said, because it was filed within three years of her having been freed and legally capable of bring the case.

Her request for an injunction against the statute of limitations defense came before the court in Hamburg on September 16, 1862. On that very day the vast armies of Confederate General Robert E. Lee and Union General George B. McClellan were preparing to fight the Battle of Antietam the following morning. It would be the bloodiest single day of the Civil War.

Judge John C. Murray was presiding in court. When the case was called, he declined to hear it. Murray had advised Abby on the case and so he was not impartial. Undoubtedly, he had advised her to go forward to court with the claim. He looked to the attorneys in the courtroom at that particular moment for someone to take the bench as judge and hear and decide the case. "Whereupon," said the court record, "the attorneys now here select from among themselves George W. Norman, Esquire, one of their number to act as special judge." It would be interesting to know whether Norman won or lost the discussion about who should be the judge. He was a 31-year-old who had practiced law for ten years in Georgia, where his father had been a judge. He did not practice in Hamburg until 1859, so he was uninvolved in the earlier litigation. He was a good choice to be the judge.

The issue to be decided by Special Judge Norman was whether Abby's claim for the seized property was barred by the statute of limitation. It was a legal question for a judge to decide and not a jury. Hutchinson argued that Abby had waited too long and could no longer sue. Waddell argued that because she was enslaved she could not sue by law until she first won her freedom, which had only recently occurred and thus the time limit did not start running until then. She had sued within three years of being freed.

It is interesting that in filing this property case Waddell did not say whether Abby was white, black or of mixed race. In the Petition for Freedom in 1855 he had said that she was white, but now in 1861 it was a place and a subject where he did not want to go. He simply said that she had been a slave and so the statute of limitations had been suspended until such time as she was declared free by a court. If he had said that Abby was white, then perhaps a judge would rule that the statute of limitation had indeed run out for reclaiming her property. If he had asserted that she was black or of mixed race, then the suit that won her freedom on the claim that she was white was a sham and she should be re-enslaved. Such a predicament left him with the best alternative of silence.

So what, then, is the truth about Abby Guy's race? The truth is that her actual racial ancestry is not now known and will never be known. Perhaps it wasn't known even then. It is accurate to say that she was overwhelmingly white. Whether she was all white or had an African ancestor can only be a subject of speculation based upon incomplete information. Her slavery or freedom depended on such distinctions. Legally, she was white because a jury set her free for that very reason. Waddell, though, was a lawyer and he wanted to get that property back for his client, so he was now silent on the question of her race in this lawsuit.

But her prior condition as a slave was well known and it was stated in the lawsuit. That a slave cannot own property of any kind,[152] and cannot sue the master except for freedom[153] were established legal principles. Special Judge Norman easily ruled for Abby, holding that her enslavement stopped the clock on the statute of limitation and that her claim now was not barred. Upon her posting of a $1,000 bond with sureties, the injunction was granted. Her attorney, John C. Waddell, and her ever faithful neighbor and friend, Richard Sanders, who had been a surety for John Arnold seven years earlier, agreed to be the sureties on the bond.[154]

After another defeat in court, Daniel's attorney, as always, said he would appeal it to the Arkansas Supreme Court. William Daniel would not accept any defeat from Abby as long as he had some avenue of appeal. By now such a thing could not have been a surprise to Abby, but this time there was no hiring out of her labor during the appeal. She was free.

The day after that court hearing, on September 17, 1862, William Daniel's son was in the Third Arkansas Regiment at the Battle of Antietam near Sharpsburg, Maryland. Word came back to Arkansas that he had been killed. He was 22 years old and had been studying law. No doubt William and Frances Daniel were devastated at the news. In her days of slavery Abby had known him as a boy and probably felt a pang of sympathy. William Daniel, on the other hand, had without mercy sought to enslave Abby's children for their entire lives.

The Arkansas Supreme Court held over in office when Arkansas joined the Confederacy. It had seen Abby Guy twice on appeal and had sustained her ultimate freedom by not overruling the verdict of the jury two years earlier. Now she was back for a third time at the court session held in June 1863. Arkansas Supreme Court business had declined during the all-out war effort of the South. Rather than the usual two-year delay, this time it was only nine months. Only twelve cases were decided that term.

During that briefer delay, however, important events were occurring. Abby's husband, David M. Roper, died some time prior to October 1862. As with James Guy and John Arnold, her marriage to older men left her a widow after only a few years. Roper, like Arnold, had been a godsend for Abby, saving her and her children from slavery during the years of appeals, hiring her labor as a means of keeping her free.

Roper's sons were sucked into the whirlwind of the increasingly desperate war, joining the Confederate military. James D. Roper enlisted as a private in the 37th Arkansas Infantry. Thomas A. Roper became a sergeant in Wright's Regiment of Arkansas Cavalry, which organized in Little Rock in the summer of 1863. There is an irony in this, of a former slave married to a man whose sons fought for the Confederacy.

On a national level, the Confederate states, including Arkansas, were beginning to collapse in the midst of war. The Union Army was in control of Fayetteville and northwest Arkansas, and also controlled Helena and other points on the Mississippi River. The siege of Vicksburg, Mississippi, was going on just sixty-five miles from Abby's home. She, however, lived in an area of undisturbed Confederate control.

On January 1, 1863, the Emancipation Proclamation of President Lincoln became effective. Its purpose was to free all slaves in the Confederate States. Slavery, however, continued to exist within Confederate lines, including Ashley County, Arkansas. Abby Guy had not waited for others to act but had self-emancipated, and she and her children were already free. Interestingly, amid this collapsing Confederate nation, a newspaper advertisement in Little Rock on June 13th said: "For Sale. A-No. 1 Negro Man, 24 years old, very likely, stout and intelligent."[155] By then, slaves and Confederate money were very poor investments for the future. People who could not read the signs of the times were still buying slaves and publishing runaway slave notices.

When the Arkansas Supreme Court met in June 1863, people in Little Rock were skittish. The future of the Confederacy was uncertain at best, and Union inroads into Arkansas were threatening. The Union Army could march on the city at any time, forcing the state government and the Supreme Court to flee.

The makeup of the Court was the same as two years earlier. Chief Justice Elbert H. English presided, with Associate Justices Hulbert F. Fairchild and Freeman W. Compton also on the bench. Robert Hutchinson represented William Daniel at the hearing. John C. Waddell, who had been admitted to Supreme Court law practice, was there for Abby, along with Augustus Garland. Garland had by then been elected to the Confederate Congress in Richmond.

It was a simple legal argument. Was Abby's claim against William Daniel for return of her property barred because she did not file suit within three years of the time he took it in 1854? Hutchinson argued that "during the pendency of Abby's suit for freedom, she was a free woman and might at any time have brought her suit."

That, of course, was utterly untrue. Garland countered that "it is well settled that a slave cannot sue except for freedom." He pointed out that Abby was not free, but had her labor continually hired out to the highest bidder. During the pendency of Abby's suit for freedom, he said, "she was treated as a slave, was to all intents and purposes a slave, was hired out, had no civil rights, and therefore could not sue." If she had sued, her case would have been dismissed because slaves cannot sue.

Garland's legal position was obviously true. Until she won her freedom, she was legally disabled from filing a lawsuit, so the three year limit didn't start running until she was declared free by the Arkansas Supreme Court in 1861. This was supported by an 1833 Tennessee Supreme Court decision. It involved a slave named Matilda who sued for freedom and won, then afterward sued the owner again for damages. Unlike Arkansas, Tennessee allowed punitive money damages against a white person for illegal enslavement of another person. The Tennessee Court held that it is a general rule that the slave cannot sue the master, so until she won her freedom case "she was imprisoned, and the statute did not run." The Tennessee court ruled in favor of Matilda, awarding her pay for her years of false imprisonment, plus fifty dollars for the expense of defeating her would-be owner's appeal of his case.[156]

After oral argument the Justices once again took the case under advisement to discuss the case and issue a written decision later. With their lightened case load and the possibility of the Union Army coming to town soon, it was probably issued much faster than had happened in the past.

When the decision came out, probably in July or August 1863, it was a bad one. The Justices were in no mood to indulge Abby Guy again, and their words had a peevish and petty tone. Justice Fairchild, the New York Yankee on the Arkansas Court, wrote a mean-spirited opinion, with Chief Justice English supporting it. They went out of their way to both repudiate Abby and embarrass Waddell.

The Justices did not like Waddell's silence on Abby's race. "Although the bill does not state whether plaintiff is a white woman, of Indian blood, or of pure or mixed African descent, it alleges she is the person whose case, under the name of Abby Guy, was twice before this court...." They noted that in the earlier trials "Abby Guy and her children claimed to be free persons solely from belonging to the white race." Now the Supreme Court made her live with that claim. "The judgment in the suit for freedom having decided the fact that Abby Guy is a white woman, it follows that she was never under any disability to sue by reason... that she was his slave." The Court's logic was that since she was later found to be white, she had always been white before, and so was never legally disabled by being a slave.[157] "She could have sued Daniel for her property when she and her children sued for themselves" for freedom, they said.

This was nonsense, using an 1861 decision to decide rights in 1855. The honorable Court knew it was nonsense. It was an example of a court badly justifying the result it wanted to reach by offering the best faulty logic it could muster. The reality was that whatever race she was in 1855 she was a slave, and legally bound by the slave code, which prevented her from suing any person for any reason except for freedom. So that was what she had done. Now they were penalizing her for it.

Then the Justices continued down the low road by ridiculing John C. Waddell, who was part of all three trials that went before the Supreme Court. It is a well known fact to attorneys, then and now, that judges sometimes take a perverse delight in embarrassing lawyers. Abby Roper, as she was called in this case, said in her documents "that she was anxious to have sued Daniel for her property, while her suit for freedom was pending, but that her counsel would not bring the suit, on the ground that she had no right to sue till her freedom should be won."

If that was Waddell's advice, the Justices sneered, "it is not the first time that this court has been obliged to differ from opinions that have been given by counsel upon the subject of litigation." Then, slamming Waddell again and complimenting themselves, they said that "mistaken advice, though injurious to the interests of the client, may not cause the courts to swerve from the correct administration of the law." These comments were not necessary to the Court's decision but were said only to hurt and embarrass.

With that reasoning, the judgment of Special Judge Norman was reversed and Abby's case for her stolen property was dismissed. Arkansas law was that William Daniel could not be sued for damages for enslaving Abby Guy and her children, and he did not have to give back the property he took from her at the time he seized them.

The Arkansas Supreme Court decision was then and is now utterly contemptible. As was intended by its authors, it must have deeply wounded Abby, but in the final analysis property was a secondary issue.

Abby Guy had already won her freedom, and no one could take that from her. That was what truly mattered.

On September 10, 1863, a few weeks after the issuance of the opinion, the authorities in Little Rock surrendered as the Union Army captured the town. Just ahead of it, the Arkansas Supreme Court fled into the countryside. Justice Hulbert F. Fairchild never sat in his Supreme Court chair in Little Rock again.

Chapter 12
Vanished

Abby Guy and her children won their freedom for several reasons. First and foremost, they won because of her own tenacious determination to be free, matched by an unconquerable spirit. She also won because under Arkansas law she had a right to a jury trial, and then had twenty-four men on two juries who supported her. In addition, she had lawyers in John C. Waddell, Benoni S. Dubose and Augustus H. Garland who willingly took on the slave establishment in court and figured out how to beat it. She also won because two trial judges let the court system work, and two Supreme Court Justices sustained the verdict of the final jury.

Abby Guy and her children would have been freed anyway, without the protracted lawsuit, in 1865 when all slaves in Ashley County were liberated at the end of the Civil War. Of course, in 1855 she had no way of knowing that was going to happen in the future, and waiting for others to free her was not Abby's way.

The problem with writing history is that it is limited by the known facts. It would be nice to say in a final chapter that Abby Guy lived a contented and pleasant life for another thirty years following the end of her legal battles. That, however, cannot be said, for not one single fact about her is known after the decision of the Arkansas Supreme Court was announced in the summer of 1863. When that opinion was issued she had already vanished from the historical record and into the mists of time.

The question arises of whether William Daniel ruined the life and personal happiness of Abby Guy. The conclusion that he wanted to ruin her life is unavoidable. Re-enslaving her at age 44, and keeping her tied up in court for six years, had a drastic impact on her life. Throwing her children into slavery made it all the worse. It gained him nothing and ultimately lost him nothing besides attorneys fees, but it cost her a great deal, not in money, but in legal enslavement, stress, emotional pain and anxiety. After fighting this monumental battle, what was her personal happiness after her legal war had been won? It is not known.

Abby was fifty years old when she finally won her freedom. How long did she live after that victory? It is not known. Abby's children, Elizabeth Frances, Mary, John and Malissa Ann, also disappeared from view. The only fact known after the end of the lawsuits is that 18-year-old Malissa Ann Arnold married 50-year-old James E. Smith in Ashley County on September 29, 1870.[158] With that age discrepancy, it seems it may have been less than a joyful occasion.

The last information known about Abby Guy personally, which occurred before the issuance of the final Arkansas Supreme Court opinion, is that on October 22, 1862, she, as "Abigail Roper," sold her interest in the land that had been owned by her late husband to his son James D. Roper. In exchange for that conveyance she received "a certain bay man mule valued at one hundred dollars."[159] One wishes to know more of the circumstances of the transaction, and why she did this. It sounds hard-working and practical, or maybe it was just plain hard. It also sounds sad. She had once owned two mares and a colt, and a yoke of oxen and a cart, but William Daniel had taken them from her because, he said, what was hers was his. Now she sold her last interest in land for a mule.

Abby's body may lie buried in a cemetery or on a farm somewhere along the bayou, and her gravestone over the years has fallen into an illegible condition. Perhaps the marker was only a wooden one which long ago disappeared. Or, perhaps, there never was a marker.

Abby Guy's mark was the one she left on history. What makes this story remarkable is not the prosperous, successful farmer and slave owner, William Daniel, but Abby Guy, the woman who would not be his slave. What became of her will perhaps one day be discovered. Hopefully, it will be that she had found a happy ending.

Undaunted
The Quiet Legacy of Abby Guy

Raised in slavery thirty years,
Tho favored, suffered; bore her tears.

Loosed to live a life full free,
Temporary dignity.

She, with children, Re-enslaved,
Vengeful master, man depraved.

Sued for Freedom, will unbent.
Grueling, galling, no relent.

By fierce tenacity obsessed,
Ownership of self she'd wrest.

Undaunted through the courts of Men,
She persevered; Slaves - n'er again!

Unleashed from historic obscurity,
Heroine of Audacity.

by Kami Garfield Mahan

Endnotes

1. Trial Record, pp. 1-4, in *Daniel v. Guy*, 19 Arkansas Supreme Court 121 (Ark. 1857). Hereinafter designated as "Trial Record." This consists of the documents prepared in 1855 and now held by the University of Arkansas Little Rock Law School Library Special Collections.

2. Trial Record, pp. 7-8.

3. Chapter 75 Freedom, Section 9, p. 551, *A Digest of the Statutes of Arkansas*, Johnson & Yerkes, State Printers, Little Rock, Arkansas, 1858. Hereinafter designated as "Statutes of Arkansas 1858."

4. *Daniel v. Guy*, 19 Arkansas Supreme Court (Ark. 1857) 121, p. 134.

5. Statutes of Arkansas 1858, Chapter 76 Free Negroes and Mulattoes, Section 1, p. 553.

6. Statutes of Arkansas 1858, Chapter 75 Freedom, Section 1, p. 550.

7. Statutes of Arkansas 1858, Chapter 75 Freedom, Section 2, p. 550.

8. Trial Record, p.10.

9. Trial Record, pp. 5-6.

10. Trial Record, p. 7.

11. Statutes of Arkansas 1858, Chapter 75 Freedom, Section 8, p. 551.

12. Trial Record, p. 13.

13. Chicot County, Arkansas, Probate Records, April 5, 1843.

14. Trial Record, p. 13.

15. *Arkansas State Gazette & Democrat*, Little Rock, August 22, 1857, p. 1.

16. *Biographical and Historical Memoirs of Southern Arkansas*, Chicago, Goodspeed Publishing Company, 1890, p. 882.

17. Trial Record, pp. 7-8.

18. *Daniel v. Roper*, 24 Arkansas Supreme Court 131 (Ark. 1863), p. 132.

19. *Matilda v. Crenshaw*, 12 Supreme Court of Errors and Appeals of Tennessee 299, (Tenn 1833).

20. *Fulton's Executors v. Gracey*, 56 Virginia Supreme Court of Appeals 314 (Va. 1859).

21. "Abraham Lincoln's comments on the Dred Scott decision in Springfield, Illinois, on June 26, 1857," *Lincoln's American Dream: Clashing Political Perspectives*, edited by Kenneth L. Deutsch and Joseph R. Fornieri, Potomoc Books, Inc., Washington, D.C., p. 51.

22. Statutes of Arkansas 1858, Chapter 51 Criminal Law, Part VI Offences Against Private Property, Article IV Enticing Away and Inciting Insurrection Among Slaves, Section 3, p. 345.

23. Statutes of Arkansas 1858, Chapter 75 Freedom, Sections 1, 2, 8, 12, 13 and 14, pp. 550-552.

24. *Chancellor v. Milly*, 39 Kentucky Court of Appeals 23 (Ky. 1839).

25. *Harris v. Clarissa,* 14 Tennessee Supreme Court 227 (Tenn. 1834).

26. *Gentry v. McMinnis,* 33 Kentucky Court of Appeals 382 (Ky. 1835).

27. *Tevis v. Eliza,* 37 Kentucky Court of Appeals 394 (Ky. 1838).

28. Twain, Mark, *Roughing It,* Hartford, American Publishing Company,1871, p. 56.

29. *The American Law Register,* Vol. 5, March 1857, edited by Asa I. Fish and Henry Wharton, Philadelphia, D.B. Canfield & Co., p. 17.

30. Statutes of Arkansas 1858, Chapter 181 Witnesses, Section 25, p. 1084-1085.

31. *Arkansas Intelligencer,* Van Buren, Arkansas, August 22, 1846, p. 3.

32. *Arkansas Intelligencer,* Van Buren, Arkansas, October 31, 1846, p. 2.

33. The counties of Chicot, Desha, Ashley, Drew, Bradley, Arkansas, Jefferson, Dallas, Hot Spring and Calhoun were in the Second Circuit. Statutes of Arkansas, Chapter 47 Courts - Circuit, Section 1, p. 303.

34. *Biographical and Historical Memoirs of Southern Arkansas,* Chicago, Goodspeed Publishing Company, 1890, p. 67.

35. "Riding the Circuit with Lincoln," Willard L. King, *American Heritage,* February 1955, Volume 6, Issue 2, p. 106.

36. *May it Please the Court: Judicial Processes and Politics in America,* Brian L. Porto, CRC Press, Boca Raton, 2008, p. 69.

37. Etheridge, Y.W., *History of Ashley County*, 1959, The Press-Argus, Van Buren, Arkansas, p. 33.

38. Ashley County, Arkansas, County Court Records, April 16, 1855.

39. *State v. Sorrels*, 15 Arkansas Supreme Court 664 (Ark. 1855).

40. Hallum, John, *Biographical and Pictorial History of Arkansas*, Volume I, Albany: Weed, Parsons and Company, 1887, pp. 305-306.

41. Statutes of Arkansas, Jurors, Chapter 98, Sections 9, 17, 22, 37, pp. 642-645.

42. Ashley County, Arkansas, County Court Records, Book A, p. 226, and U.S. Census, Ashley County, Arkansas, 1850 and 1860.

43. Trial Record, p. 16.

44. Trial Record, p. 20.

45. U.S. Census, Ashley County, Arkansas, 1850 and 1860.

46. United States Bureau of Land Management, General Land Office Automated Records Project, Ashley County, Arkansas.

47. Trial Record, p. 16.

48. Trial record, p. 21.

49. U.S. Census, Ashley County, Arkansas, 1850.

50. Trial Record, p. 21.

51. Statutes of Arkansas 1858, Chapter 109 Marriages, Section 4, p. 760.

52. U.S. Census, Ashley County, Arkansas, 1840.

53. United States Bureau of Land Management, General Land Office Automated Records Project, Ashley County, Arkansas.

54. U.S. Census, Ashley County, Arkansas, 1850.

55. Statutes of Arkansas 1858, Chapter 162 Slaves, Section 61, p. 1035.

56. Trial Record, p. 20.

57. *Fulton's Executors v. Gracey*, 56 Virginia Supreme Court of Appeals 314 (Va. 1859).

58. *Gentry v. McMinnis*, 33 Kentucky Court of Appeals 382 (Ky. 1835).

59. *Chancellor v. Milly*, 39 Kentucky Court of Appeals 23 (Ky. 1839).

60. *Gentry v. McMinnis*, 33 Kentucky Court of Appeals 382 (Ky. 1835).

61. Trial Record, p. 21.

62. *Arkansas Whig*, Little Rock, Thursday, May 24, 1855.

63. Trial Record, pp. 21-22.

64. U.S. Census, Slave Schedules, Ashley County, Arkansas, 1850.

65. Trial Record, p. 22.

66. Trial Record, p. 22.

67. Trial Record, p. 23.

68. *General Act Providing for the Census of 1850*, U.S. Congress, p. XIX.

69. Trial Record, p. 23.

70. Etheridge, Y.W., *History of Ashley County*, 1959, The Press-Argus, Van Buren, Arkansas, pp. 84-85.

71. Trial Record, pp. 23-24.

72. Trial Record, pp. 16 and 24.

73. Trial Record, pp. 24-25.

74. *Biographical and Historical Memoirs of Southern Arkansas*, Chicago, Goodspeed Publishing Company, 1890, p. 897.

75. *Biographical and Historical Memoirs of Southern Arkansas*, Chicago, Goodspeed Publishing Company, 1890, p. 874.

76. Ashley County, Arkansas, County Court Records, April 17, April 30 and July 16, 1849.

77. Trial Record, pp. 64-68.

78. *Wood v. Humphreys*, 53 Virginia Supreme Court of Appeals 333 (Va. 1855).

79. *Harris v. Clarissa*, 14 Supreme Court of Errors and Appeals of Tennessee 227 (Tenn. 1834).

80. *Report of the Research Committee on Thomas Jefferson and Sally Hemings*, Thomas Jefferson Foundation, January 2000, Section IV, Research Findings and Implications.

81. Statutes of Arkansas 1858, Chapter 76 Free Negroes and Mulattoes, Section 1, p. 553.

82. Trial Record, p. 2.

83. Zanita E. Fenton, *An Essay on Slavery's Hidden Legacy: Social Hysteria and Structural Condonation of Incest*, 55Howard L.J.319 (2012).

84. Trial Record, pp. 25-26.

85. Trial Record, pp. 27-28.

86. Trial Record, pp. 25-28.

87. Trial Record, pp. 28-29.

88. Trial Record, p. 29.

89. Trial Record, pp. 29-30.

90. Trial Record, p. 30.

91. Trial Record, p. 31.

92. Trial Record, p. 34.

93. Trial Record p. 50.

94. Trial Record, pp. 52-59.

95. Trial Record, pp. 61-62.

96. Trial Record, pp. 62-63.

97. Trial Record, pp. 59-61.

98. Trial Record, p. 16.

99. *Pleasant v. State*, 13 Arkansas Supreme Court 360 (Ark. 1853).

100. *Biographical and Historical Memoirs of Southern Arkansas*, Chicago, Goodspeed Publishing Company, 1890, pp. 874-875.

101. Trial Record, p. 16.

102. Trial Record, pp 16-17.

103. Trial Record, pp. 17-19.

104. Trial Record, pp. 19-20.

105. Statutes of Arkansas 1858, Chapter 109 Marriages, Section 4, p. 760.

106. *Jackson v. Bob*, 18 Arkansas Supreme Court 399 (Ark 1857).

107. *Dred Scott v. Sanford*, 60 US 393 (United States Supreme Court 1857).

108. *Pendleton v. The State*, 6 Arkansas Supreme Court 509 (Ark. 1846).

109. *Arkansas State Gazette & Democrat*, Little Rock, October 31, 1857, p. 4.

110. *Arkansas State Gazette & Democrat*, Little Rock, July 18, 1857, p. 2.

111. *The Encyclopedia of Arkansas History and Culture* entry on Christopher Columbus Scott, an online service of the Central Arkansas Library System, www.encyclopediaofarkansas.net.

112. *Arkansas State Gazette & Democrat*, Little Rock, September 12, 1857, p.2.

113. *Daniel v. Guy*, 19 Arkansas Supreme Court 121 (Ark. 1857), p. 138.

114. Ashley County, Arkansas, Circuit Court Records, Book B, p. 310.

115. *Daniel v. Guy*, 23 Arkansas Supreme Court 50 (Ark 1861), p. 130.

116. *Daniel v. Guy*, 23 Arkansas Supreme Court 50 (Ark 1861), p. 134.

117. Statutes of Arkansas 1858, Chapter 75 Freedom, Section 12, p. 552, and Chapter 76 Free Negroes and Mulattoes, Section 1, p. 553.

118. L. Scott Stafford, *Slavery and the Arkansas Supreme Court*, 19 U. Ark. Little Rock Law Review 413 (1997), p. 460.

119. Statutes of Arkansas 1858, Chapter 75 Freedom, Section 8, p. 551.

120. Statutes of Arkansas 1858, Chapter 109 Marriages, Section 4, p. 760.

121. Ashley County, Arkansas, Marriage Records, Book AA, 1837-1871, p. 99.

122. *Gary v. Stevenson*, 19 Arkansas Supreme Court 580 (Ark. 1858).

123. *Bob v. Powers*, 19 Arkansas Supreme Court 424 (Ark. 1858).

124. *Arkansas State Gazette & Democrat*, Little Rock, August 22, 1857, p. 1.

125. Drew County, Arkansas, Circuit Court Records, Book C, pp. 264-265.

126. *Arkansas State Gazette & Democrat*, Little Rock, April 24, 1839, p. 4.

127. Drew County, Arkansas, Circuit Court Records, Book C, p. 95.

128. Drew County, Arkansas, Circuit Court Records, Book C, p. 98.

129. Drew County, Arkansas, Circuit Court Records, Book C, p. 151.

130. Drew County, Arkansas, Circuit Court Records, Book C, pp. 151-152.

131. Arkansas Legislature, Act 151, 1859.

132. Drew County, Arkansas, Circuit Court Records, Book C, p. 265.

133. Drew County, Arkansas, Circuit Court Records, Book B, p. 438.

134. Drew County, Arkansas, Circuit Court Records, Book C, p. 265.

135. Drew County, Arkansas, Circuit Court Records, Book C, p. 265.

136. Drew County, Arkansas, Circuit Court Records, Book C, pp. 270-271.

137. Drew County, Arkansas, Circuit Court Records, Book C, p. 299.

138. Drew County, Arkansas, Circuit Court Records, Book C, p. 301.

139. Drew County, Arkansas, Circuit Court Records, Book C, p. 365.

140. *Daniel v. Guy*, 23 Arkansas Supreme Court 50 (Ark 1861), p. 54.

141. Drew County, Arkansas, Circuit Court Records, Book C, p. 366.

142. *Daniel v. Guy*, 23 Arkansas Supreme Court 50 (Ark 1861), p. 54.

143. *Daniel v. Guy*, 23 Arkansas Supreme Court 50 (Ark 1861), p. 54.

144. *Stewart v. State*, 13 Arkansas Supreme Court 720 (Ark. 1853).

145. *Collier v. State*, 20 Arkansas Supreme Court 36 (Ark. 1859).

146. *Daniel v. Guy*, 23 Arkansas Supreme Court 50 (Ark 1861), p. 54.

147. Drew County, Arkansas, Circuit Court Records, Book C, p. 366.

148. *Arkansas State Gazette*, Little Rock, pp. 1-2.

149. *Daniel v. Guy*, 23 Arkansas Supreme Court 50 (Ark 1861), p. 52.

150. Arkansas Statutes 1858, Freedom, Chapter 75, Section 14, p. 552.

151. *Daniel v. Roper*, 24 Arkansas Supreme Court 131 (Arkansas 1863), p. 132.

152. *Harris v. Clarissa*, 14 Tennessee Court of Errors and Appeals 227 (Tenn. 1834).

153. *Matilda v. Crenshaw*, 12 Tennessee Court of Errors and Appeals 299 (Tenn. 1833).

154. Ashley County, Arkansas, Circuit Court Records, Book A, pp. 302-303.

155. *Arkansas State Gazette*, Little Rock, Arkansas, June 13, 1863, p. 2.

156. *Matilda v. Crenshaw*, 12 Court of Errors and Appeals of Tennessee 299 (Tenn. 1833).

157. *Daniel v. Roper*, 24 Arkansas Supreme Court 131 (Arkansas 1863), p. 131.

158. Ashley County, Arkansas, Marriage Index, 1870.

159. Ashley County, Arkansas, Deed Book F, p. 74.

Partial Bibliography

This book is based upon original research in the following primary documents:

1. The handwritten pages in the 1855 documents in the Arkansas Supreme Court case of *Daniel v. Guy*, 19 Arkansas Supreme Court 121 (Ark. 1857) held by the Arkansas History Commission and the Arkansas State Archives in Little Rock, Arkansas. My thanks to Kathryn Fitzhugh for making this trial record available to me.

2. The handwritten pages of court records and county records from 1848 to 1863 held by the Ashley County Circuit Clerk in Hamburg, Arkansas, and the Drew County Circuit Clerk in Monticello, Arkansas. My thanks to the very helpful clerks of these offices.

3. The Arkansas Supreme Court decisions in the cases of *Daniel v. Guy*, 19 Arkansas Supreme Court 121 (1857), *Daniel v. Guy*, 23 Arkansas Supreme Court 50 (1861), and *Daniel v. Roper*, 24 Arkansas Supreme Court 131 (1863).

4. The 1856 laws of Arkansas as published in *A Digest of the Statutes of Arkansas*, Johnson & Yerkes, State Printers, Little Rock, Arkansas, 1858.

5. The pre-Civil War decisions of Southern state Supreme Courts in slave freedom lawsuits, as individually referenced in the text and in the Endnotes.

6. The handwritten pages of the U.S. Census records for 1840, 1850 and 1860 in Arkansas and other states, available from numerous sources.

7. Contemporaneous (1840-1863) newspaper accounts in the *Arkansas State Gazette & Democrat* in Little Rock, the *Arkansas Intelligencer* in Van Buren, and the *Arkansas Whig* in Little Rock.

8. Land records from 1840 to 1863 for Ashley County, Arkansas, held by the United States Bureau of Land Management, and made available in the General Land Office Automated Records Project.

Numerous secondary sources have been consulted, many of which are cited in the Endnotes.

Index

Made in the USA
Monee, IL
01 April 2026

47384191R00079